My friend Amanda̶ ̶
trality of the prop̶ ̶
church and beautifully lives that out in her own life. I
am so grateful she has put pen to paper and that she—
and Donné Clement Petruska in this book—have given
us the benefit of their grounded and biblical wisdom.
May God use this book in the life of everyone who
reads it!

—ERIC METAXAS
AUTHOR, *BONHOEFFER*, *MIRACLES*, and *IS ATHEISM
DEAD?*; HOST, *SOCRATES IN THE CITY* AND
THE ERIC METAXAS SHOW

I appreciate the way both Amanda and Kim's daughter
Donné honor Kim Clement in this book. I traveled
with Kim and believe he would wholeheartedly say
amen to his daughter and agree with Amanda's prophetic description of America from 2008 to the present.
There are hidden gems in here for every lover of the
prophetic, both the seasoned warrior and the new
recruit. Amanda has given us a valuable contribution
to understanding prophecy.

—LANCE WALLNAU
SPEAKER; AUTHOR; CEO, LANCE LEARNING GROUP

Amanda Grace is a God-inspired teacher who has
helped reawaken millions to the never-changing truth
found in the irrefutable Word of God, known as the
Bible. I highly recommend that you invest the time to
discover her ministry, her broadcasts, and this book!

—CLAY CLARK
FOUNDER, REAWAKEN AMERICA TOUR; HOST,
THE THRIVETIME SHOW; FORMER OKLAHOMA
ENTREPRENEUR OF THE YEAR

The Revelationary War is not only timely, it is profoundly accurate in demonstrating decades of prophetic and biblical connections within our nation, Israel, and the church, linking serious events that have occurred over time. We have been in an epic battle for the soul and freedom of this nation that affects the world and the church.

This book dives into the great plumb line the Lord over time has been dropping within the church between the true shepherds and the showmen and demonstrates how prophetic events within the political arena have also run parallel and occurred within the church. Considering that we have just endured a profound year and election within the United States, Amanda Grace makes incredible connections going back to the formation of our great nation.

This book shines a spotlight on prophecy and shows readers how to truly understand and discern the prophetic from the deceptions the enemy and his agents have attempted to saturate the airwaves, media, and church with—their own revelations that oppose the Lord, His Word, and His will. We truly are in a revelationary war, a battle of the ages. I so appreciate that Amanda Grace answered the call from the Lord and chose to help fight this war and through this book continues to equip the church!

—Lt. Gen. Michael Flynn, Retired,
Former National Security Advisor

Jesus says to us in Matthew 24:4, "Take heed that no one deceives you," in the New King James Version. But all the versions say the same thing: Let no one, no man, nothing deceive, mislead, or lead you astray. They are all telling us we need to be on the watch so we're not fooled by the wiles of the devil. For someone who knew the end from the beginning, I think the Lord knew what He was talking about. It was the devil's big hit, his original deceiving plan to get Adam and Eve to go against what God had told them not to do. "But of the tree of the knowledge of good and evil, you shall not eat. For the day that you eat of it, you shall surely die" (Gen. 2:17)—and we've been dying ever since.

In *The Revelationary War*, Amanda Grace has diagnosed the condition of many in the body of Christ, and like any good doctor, she's given us the right antidote for our sickness: Take a hefty dose of God's Word every day, drink it down with a glass of the Holy Spirit, and do it as often as you can. You can't take too much, so take it often. It's the only antidote known to mankind that can kill the venom from the serpent of old. When Amanda speaks, I listen.

—RICKY SKAGGS
COUNTRY AND BLUEGRASS SINGER, MUSICIAN,
PRODUCER, COMPOSER

THE
REVELATIONARY
WAR

THE
REVELATIONARY
WAR

AMANDA GRACE

 CHARISMA HOUSE

THE REVELATIONARY WAR by Amanda Grace
Published by Charisma House, an imprint of Charisma Media
1150 Greenwood Blvd., Lake Mary, Florida 32746

for changes that occur after publication. Further, the publisher and author do not have any control over and do not assume any responsibility for third-party websites or their content.

For more resources like this, visit MyCharismaShop.com and the author's website at arkofgrace.org.

Cataloging-in-Publication Data is on file with the Library of Congress.
International Standard Book Number: 978-1-63641-432-4
E-book ISBN: 978-1-63641-433-1

01 2025
Printed in the United States of America

Most Charisma Media products are available at special quantity discounts for bulk purchase for sales promotions, premiums, fund-raising, and educational needs. For details, call us at (407) 333-0600 or visit our website at charismamedia.com.

CONTENTS

INTRODUCTION

ELP ME, LORD, bring glory to Your name first and bring what You want to come forth, in Jesus' name. Praise be to the name of the Lord Most High!

This book was brought about by almighty God through the obedience of a Texas pastor. A friend of mine was obedient to the Lord when he had a God-given dream. In that dream the Lord told him, "Amanda is to write a book called *The Revelationary War*," and I was to call upon Donné Clement Petruska, daughter of Kim Clement, to contribute. This book is divinely given and guided to expose truth and be a light in an hour of such deception. To God be all the glory!

In this current day and age on the earth, we find ourselves in the midst of a revelationary war unlike any other, a war between true prophets of the Lord and false prophets. The church, the body of Christ, has allowed the words of serpents to divide us, to separate us, and to cause disunity by placing false prophecies above the Word of God. In this modern digital age it is a war being fought through media, through the powers of the air. And the prophets of Baal are completely given over to weaving deceptions into the minds of both the young and the old. In this revelationary war true prophets, true servants of God, and true ministers of the fivefold ministry have found themselves facing a multiheaded beast from the abyss.

The attack on prophecy is an attack on the truth. We must now, under the Lord's instruction, go back to, face, and overcome what is poised to defeat us. You must know the truth to recognize what is false. To fully understand the different fronts of this war and what we as believers in Christ must do to be victors over the enemy, we must be grounded in the truth.

CHAPTER 1

WHAT IS PROPHECY?

WHAT IS PROPHECY? Well, to some that is a loaded question. However, we are going to answer that question in this chapter. Amos 3:7 states, "Surely the Lord GOD does nothing without revealing His secret plan [of the judgment to come] to His servants the prophets." Prophecy is not just about revealing and revelation—it is an announcement of the thoughts, plans, purposes, and judgments of God.

In Genesis 1:29 God said to Adam, "Behold, I have given you every plant yielding seed that is on the surface of the entire earth, and every tree which has fruit yielding seed; it shall be food for you." The fifth letter of the Hebrew alphabet is *heh*. It means behold; it refers to an announcement. So when God told Adam to *behold*, He was saying, "This is My announcement. These are My thoughts and plans for you." It was a revelation of what God was doing and planning, an announcement of instruction to Adam about what he and his family could eat.

God also told Adam, "You may freely (unconditionally) eat [the fruit] from every tree of the garden; but [only] from the tree of the knowledge (recognition) of good and evil you shall not eat, otherwise on the day that you eat from it, you shall most certainly die [because of your disobedience]" (Gen. 2:16–17). This statement was an announcement of instruction from God about everything that was allowed and one little thing that wasn't, and it was also an announcement about the potential judgment if Adam chose to disobey God.

So at its most basic, prophecy is an announcement from God. It can contain instructions, plans, encouragements, judgments, blessings, revelations, and anything else that God wants to announce to His people.

WHAT PROPHECY AND PROPHETS ARE NOT

Before we look further at what prophecy and prophets are, let's look at what they are not.

Prophets are not fortune tellers or psychics or witches or anything similar in the occult realm. I am going to make that distinction for you here. To help you understand and give you a clear mental image, I want you to think about the movie *Star Wars*. A key concept in the film is the force. There is a good side to the force, and there is a very bad, or dark, side to the force. The force and the abilities it gives can be utilized for good or for evil.[1]

It is the same with the gift of prophecy. Romans 11:29 says, "For the gifts and the calling of God are irrevocable [for He does not withdraw what He has given, nor does He change His mind about those to whom He gives His grace or to whom He sends His call]." God gives gifts to us all, and it is our choice to use those gifts for good or for evil. God doesn't take the gift back just because someone goes rogue and doesn't use it the way God intended it to be used.

Psychics, fortune tellers, and witches get their information and instructions from the kingdom of darkness. Although there are many who claim that is not true, it is true. Many of these people involved in the occult are prophets gone rogue, meaning that the gifts and abilities they have were present when they were created by God. Their gifts were in them from birth, but Satan hijacked them and took them for his own destructive purposes.

The information of psychics, fortune tellers, and witches comes from things called familiar spirits. They are called familiar spirits because they are familiar with everything about you—your family lines, your strengths, your weaknesses, your gifts, your challenges, your struggles, and so forth. They know *you*. They study people through the generations, and their goal is to get man's eyes off the Lord and get man instead to trust and have faith in an adulterated, corrupt power that comes from the kingdom of darkness. When they succeed with their goal, they then are able to put that generation into cyclical bondages that continue rather than break.

Prophet Kim Clement would say the words may be right, but the breath is wrong. What that means is the words these occultists and mediums speak to you may have some truth to them, but any truth is mixed with a whole lot of lie. Also, the source from which that "truth" comes is the kingdom of darkness. Satan is trying to use his kingdom of darkness to ultimately enslave and destroy humanity, separating them from almighty God for eternity.

The Book of Acts has a perfect example of this.

> It happened that as we were on our way to the place of prayer, we were met by a slave-girl who had a spirit of divination [that is, a demonic spirit claiming to foretell the future and discover hidden knowledge], and she brought her owners a good profit by fortune-telling. She followed after Paul and us and kept screaming and shouting, "These men are servants of the Most High God! They are proclaiming to you the way of salvation!" She continued doing this for several days. Then

> Paul, being greatly annoyed and worn out, turned and said to the spirit [inside her], "I command you in the name of Jesus Christ [as His representative] to come out of her!" And it came out at that very moment.
>
> —ACTS 16:16–18

What the girl shouted is correct—Paul and Timothy were "servants of the Most High God," and they were proclaiming the way of salvation. The words were right, but the breath, the source from which the words came, was very wrong! *The source matters.* This is why in the prophetic our source *must* be the Lord. We must make sure we are drinking from a pure well, because when other fallible and fleshly things are added, it taints the well.

Another example of this is when Jesus faced Satan head-on in the wilderness after fasting forty days and forty nights. When Jesus was at His weakest, the enemy came to attack Him. In that exchange between Jesus Christ and Satan the enemy was tempting Jesus to do something that would be for His harm and all humanity's harm as well.

Satan and his kingdom look to exploit your weaknesses, for when they can exploit your weaknesses, they can ensnare your strengths. Satan tried it with Jesus, and he will try it with you too.

> Then the devil took Him into the holy city [Jerusalem] and placed Him on the pinnacle (highest point) of the temple. And he said [mockingly] to Him, "If You are the Son of God, throw Yourself down; for it is written, 'He will command His angels concerning You [to serve, care for, protect and watch over You]'; and 'They will lift you up on their hands, so that You will not strike Your foot against a stone.'"
>
> —MATTHEW 4:5–6

Again, the words are correct. Satan was quoting the Word of God, and Psalm 91 does say those things—but the breath was wrong; the source was wrong. The source was dark and intent on destruction. Satan was misusing the Word of God for his own purposes.

However, Jesus answered, "On the other hand, it is written and forever remains written, 'You shall not test the Lord your God'" (Matt. 4:7). Jesus quoted Deuteronomy 6:16, and not only were the words correct, but the source was also right, and it was truth. When someone tests God, it brings them harm. The enemy was utilizing the Word of God to tempt and bring harm. We are kidding ourselves if we do not realize Satan knows Scripture and has been attempting since the Garden of Eden to use the Word of God in an illegal and perverse way to bring destruction upon man.

Another example of the perversion of spiritual power is in the story of the witch of En-dor.

> Then Saul said to his servants, "Find for me a woman who is a medium [between the living and the dead], so that I may go to her and ask her advice." His servants said to him, "There is a woman who is a medium at En-dor."
>
> So Saul disguised himself by wearing different clothes, and he left with two men, and they came to the woman at night. He said to her, "Conjure up for me, please, and bring up [from the dead] for me [the spirit] whom I shall name to you." But the woman said to him, "See here, you know what Saul has done, how he has cut off (eliminated) those who are mediums and spiritists from the land. So why are you laying a trap for my life, to cause my death?" Then Saul swore [an oath] to her by the LORD, saying, "As the LORD lives, no punishment shall come

upon you for this." So the woman said, "Whom shall I bring up for you?" He said, "Bring up Samuel for me." When the woman saw Samuel, she screamed with a loud voice; and she said to Saul, "Why have you deceived me? You are Saul!" The king said to her, "Do not be afraid; but [tell me] what do you see?" The woman said to Saul, "I see a divine [superhuman] being coming up from the earth." He said to her, "What is his appearance?" And she said, "An old man is coming up, wrapped in a robe." Then Saul knew that it was Samuel, and he bowed with his face to the ground and paid respect [to him].

—1 SAMUEL 28:7–14

Saul, a once righteous king, sought out the kingdom of darkness to find an answer that the Lord had. Saul knew first-hand how the Lord could be relied on, and the Spirit of God had come upon him more than once. However, he began to rebel against the Lord and His Word. Saul strayed so far out from under the covering of the Lord that in desperation he sought the antithesis of God and His truth. Prophecy truly can be a fine line because the source matters very much.

THE GIFT OF PROPHECY

When the apostle Paul was instructing the believers in Rome about how the body of Christ was to operate, he wrote,

For just as in one [physical] body we have many parts, and these parts do not all have the same function or special use, so we, who are many, are [nevertheless just] one body in Christ, and individually [we are] parts one of another [mutually dependent on each other]. Since we have gifts that differ according to the grace given to us, each of us is to use them accordingly: if [someone has the gift of] prophecy, [let him speak a new message from God to His people] in proportion to the faith possessed; if service, in the act of serving; or he who teaches, in the act of teaching; or he who encourages, in the act of encouragement; he who gives, with generosity; he who leads, with diligence; he who shows mercy [in caring for others], with cheerfulness.

—ROMANS 12:4–8

Within the context of the body of Christ, prophecy can be delivered either through someone with the gift of prophecy or by someone with the office of prophet. The gift of prophecy and the office of prophet are distinctly different.

God gives different spiritual gifts to believers for the purpose of building, strengthening, and encouraging His body. All believers have the potential to move in the gift of prophecy. A believer with the gift of prophecy is to use it accordingly, to speak the message given from God to His people.

When the prophet Samuel anointed Saul as king of Israel, Samuel prophesied that Saul himself would prophesy when the Spirit of the Lord would come upon him while he encountered a company of prophets. And that is exactly what happened.

Then it happened when Saul turned his back to leave Samuel, God changed his heart; and all those signs came to pass that day. When they came to the hill [Gibeah], behold, a group of prophets met him; and the Spirit of God came on him mightily, and he prophesied [under divine guidance] among them.

—1 SAMUEL 10:9–10

Although Saul was not a prophet, he prophesied at a time when God gave him the gift of prophecy. This shows us that God can use anyone. All believers have the potential to operate or move in the gift of prophecy.

But Saul's prophesying also shows us that just because someone was given the gift of prophecy at one time and prophesied accurately by the Spirit of God does not mean that we can take everything they say as being true and inspired by God. For as we just learned, Saul eventually rebelled against God and turned to the kingdom of darkness as his source. That is why Paul told us to "pay attention and weigh carefully what is said" (1 Cor. 14:29).

The Lord moves on different people at different times, and depending on what the Holy Spirit shows them, they may give words of knowledge, words of wisdom, or even foretellings or forewarnings of future events. Prophecies can also be words of edification, encouragement, or consolation.

> But [on the other hand] the one who prophesies speaks to people for edification [to promote their spiritual growth] and [speaks words of] encouragement [to uphold and advise them concerning the matters of God] and [speaks words of] consolation [to compassionately comfort them]. One who speaks in a tongue edifies himself; but one who prophesies edifies the church [promotes growth in spiritual wisdom, devotion, holiness, and joy].
> —1 CORINTHIANS 14:3–4

The apostle Paul wrote that we should especially desire and cultivate the gift of prophecy: "Pursue [this] love [with eagerness, make it your goal], yet earnestly desire and cultivate the spiritual gifts [to be used by believers for the benefit of the church], but especially that you may prophesy [to foretell the future, to speak a new message from God to the people]" (1 Cor. 14:1). He also wrote,

> Now I wish that all of you spoke in unknown tongues,
> but even more [I wish] that you would prophesy. The
> one who prophesies is greater [and more useful] than
> the one who speaks in tongues, unless he translates or
> explains [what he says], so that the church may be edi-
> fied [instructed, improved, strengthened].
>
> —1 Corinthians 14:5

One of the purposes of prophecy is to edify the church. *Merriam-Webster* defines that to *edify* is "to instruct and improve especially in moral and religious knowledge; uplift, enlighten, inform."[2] The Greek word for *edify* in 1 Corinthians 14 means to build, to build up, "to restore by building," to establish, to embolden, and to promote spiritual growth.[3] Clearly, prophecy is of benefit to the church, to the body of Christ. First Corinthians 14:31 says, "You can all prophesy one by one, so that everyone may be instructed and everyone may be encouraged."

THE OFFICE OF PROPHET

The office of prophet is very different from the gift of prophecy. Individuals who hold the office of prophet are born into it. At a very young age, in an unharnessed way, they begin to operate in it, whether it is through visions, dreams, or words coming forth from them that they are too young to fully understand at the time. We know this to be true because of what God said to the prophet Jeremiah when He first called him.

> Now the word of the LORD came to me, saying, "Before
> I formed you in the womb I knew you [and approved
> of you as My chosen instrument], and before you were

born I consecrated you [to Myself as My own]; I have appointed you as a prophet to the nations."

—Jeremiah 1:4–5

The office of prophet is part of the fivefold ministry. Ephesians 4:11–16 (nkjv) says,

> And He Himself gave some to be apostles, some prophets, some evangelists, and some pastors and teachers, for the equipping of the saints for the work of ministry, for the edifying of the body of Christ, till we all come to the unity of the faith and of the knowledge of the Son of God, to a perfect man, to the measure of the stature of the fullness of Christ; that we should no longer be children, tossed to and fro and carried about with every wind of doctrine, by the trickery of men, in the cunning craftiness of deceitful plotting, but, speaking the truth in love, may grow up in all things into Him who is the head—Christ—from whom the whole body, joined and knit together by what every joint supplies, according to the effective working by which every part does its share, causes growth of the body for the edifying of itself in love.

The office of prophet is a much heavier, weightier anointing or responsibility than the gift of prophecy. The words and the teachings go much deeper. They do not stay on the surface but rather enable and equip believers to grow deeper roots and come into a deeper understanding with the Lord. When this occurs, the fruit of spiritual and emotional maturity grows.

As I said, prophecy truly can be a fine line because the source very much matters. Prophecy needs to come from a pure stream of God and His words to be accurate, to be powerful, and to accomplish what the Lord has proclaimed.

Then the LORD came down in the cloud and spoke to him; and He took some of the Spirit who was upon Moses and put Him upon the seventy elders. When the Spirit rested upon them, they prophesied [praising God and declaring His will], but they did not do it again.

But two men had remained in the camp; one named Eldad and the other named Medad. The Spirit rested upon them (now they were among those who had been registered, but had not gone out to the Tent), and they prophesied in the camp. So a young man ran and told Moses and said, "Eldad and Medad are prophesying [extolling the praises of God and declaring His will] in the camp." Then Joshua the son of Nun, the attendant of Moses from his youth, said, "My lord Moses, stop them!" But Moses said to him, "Are you jealous for my sake? Would that all the LORD's people were prophets and that the LORD would put His Spirit upon them!"

—NUMBERS 11:25–29

When a prophet declares God's will, it has to come from the source of almighty God. It is then announced to the people. That is how prophecy should operate—it comes from God and then is delivered to the people. And for it to operate with the precision and accuracy that it should, the one prophesying must keep their vessel as pure as possible. If one is constantly filling their soul with dark rabbit holes and junk intel and certain TV shows, movies, radio programs, podcasts, and the like, it corrupts the vessel. When one's vessel is corrupted, it means the enemy is given an easier chance to sound similar to God and actually trick that individual into speaking where the breath is wrong, the source is contaminated, and the words are superficial. This leads people away from the Lord. Prophecy should always point people back to the Lord.

If a prophet arises among you, or a dreamer of dreams, and gives you a sign or a wonder, and the sign or the wonder which he spoke (foretold) to you comes to pass, and if he says, "Let us follow after other gods (whom you have not known) and let us serve and worship them," you shall not listen to the words of that prophet or that dreamer of dreams; for the LORD your God is testing you to know whether you love the LORD your God with all your heart and mind and all your soul [your entire being]. You shall walk after the LORD your God and you shall fear [and worship] Him [with awe-filled reverence and profound respect], and you shall keep His commandments and you shall listen to His voice, and you shall serve Him, and cling to Him.

—DEUTERONOMY 13:1–4

Prophets are tools and vessels in the hands of an infinitely powerful God, and prophets are meant to point people back to the Lord, to bring in the fear of the Lord—which is the beginning of wisdom (Prov. 9:10)—and to draw people into closer relationship with the Lord. Prophets are meant to teach as well; the prophetic office, or the prophetic mantle, holds a teaching anointing.

Prophets are not meant to point people back to junk intel or to make people obsessed with the news. Yes, events that are spoken forth may be reported; however, there should always be a steering back to the Lord.

Prophets are not meant to be cheerleaders either. As I mentioned, the office of prophet carries a weight, a heavy weight of truth and responsibility. There are times prophets have to say very difficult things because the stakes are high—sometimes even a nation is at stake—and leaders who have been positioned for specific purposes are about to falter. The power of the truth of God can bring things back in order and give a much-needed hard correction.

In the Scriptures, Nathan was a prophet who had to speak difficult truth on more than one occasion. Nathan was an adviser to King David. As David grew in power and influence, he faced more and more temptation, and he eventually gave in.

Second Samuel 11 tells about the time King David was walking on the roof of his palace and saw a woman, Bathsheba, bathing. Now, David already had many wives, but he gave in to the temptation presented before his eyes. David abused his power as king and took Bathsheba, who was married to Uriah the Hittite, and had sexual relations with her. She became pregnant, and in an attempt to cover up his sin, David had Uriah killed in battle. David then took Bathsheba as his wife.

Enter Nathan the prophet. The Lord exposed to Nathan what David had done.

Nathan privately went to David because the sin that was committed was so serious it teetered on costing David the nation and on David and Bathsheba being dealt with according to the Law. Nathan understood the gravity of the situation and that the nation teetered on the brink of losing its king to the penalty for sin.

Nathan told David an account of a rich man who had many sheep and a poor man who had one little lamb that he loved. The rich man took the poor man's lamb and killed it to feed his guest, even though he had many of his own sheep to choose from. Then came the point when Nathan, in the office of prophet, delivered to David the decision of the Lord, the judgment handed down from the court of almighty God. After Nathan finished telling David the story, 2 Samuel says,

> Then David's anger burned intensely against the man, and he said to Nathan, "As the LORD lives, the man who

has done this deserves to die. He shall make restitution for the ewe lamb four times as much [as the lamb was worth], because he did this thing and had no compassion."

Then Nathan said to David, "You are the man! Thus says the LORD, the God of Israel, 'I anointed you as king over Israel, and I spared you from the hand of Saul. I also gave you your master's house, and put your master's wives into your care and under your protection, and I gave you the house (royal dynasty) of Israel and of Judah; and if that had been too little, I would have given you much more! Why have you despised the word of the LORD by doing evil in His sight? You have struck down Uriah the Hittite with the sword and have taken his wife to be your wife. You have killed him with the sword of the Ammonites. Now, therefore, the sword shall never depart from your house, because you have despised Me and have taken the wife of Uriah the Hittite to be your wife.' Thus says the LORD, 'Behold, I will stir up evil against you from your own household; and I will take your wives before your eyes and give them to your companion, and he will lie with your wives in broad daylight. Indeed you did it secretly, but I will do this thing before all Israel, and in broad daylight.'" David said to Nathan, "I have sinned against the LORD." And Nathan said to David, "The LORD also has allowed your sin to pass [without further punishment]; you shall not die. Nevertheless, because by this deed you have given [a great] opportunity to the enemies of the LORD to blaspheme [Him], the son that is born to you shall certainly die." Then Nathan went [back] to his home.

—2 SAMUEL 12:5–15

That man is you, David! This was the king of Israel whom Nathan was speaking to. However, prophets fear God more than they fear man and what man will say or do to them, even when the man is a king. At that moment, Nathan had a critical assignment to do in an attempt to save David from losing his seat in leadership and to save Israel as a nation from being thrown into chaos.

Prophets do not pander to man—we speak the word of the Lord because that is what we are trained up to do. It is why we are refined and tested: "For You have tested us, O God; You have refined us as silver is refined" (Ps. 66:10). A word of the Lord is like a fire in your bones; it has to be spoken because you can't hold it inside. Jeremiah 20:9 says, "If I say, 'I will not remember Him or speak His name anymore,' then my heart becomes a burning fire shut up in my bones. And I am weary of enduring and holding it in; I cannot endure it [nor contain it any longer]."

Prophets carry the authority that only almighty God can give! There is an authority that proceeds from their voices, and there is a depth to what they say. When prophets write or speak the word of the Lord, there is a revealing, a revelation that takes place to edify, to rebuke, to exalt, and to warn of coming events.

Prophets are meant as well to expose the plans of the enemy as those plans are set in motion so they can be dismantled and destroyed.

> Now the king of Aram (Syria) was making war against Israel, and he consulted with his servants, saying, "My camp shall be in such and such a place." The man of God [Elisha] sent word to the king of Israel saying, "Be careful not to pass by this place, because the Arameans are pulling back to there." Then the king of Israel sent word to the place about which Elisha had warned him; so he guarded himself there repeatedly.

> Now the heart of the king of Aram (Syria) was enraged over this thing. He called his servants and said to them, "Will you not tell me which of us is helping the king of Israel?" One of his servants said, "None [of us is helping him], my lord, O king; but Elisha, the prophet who is in Israel, tells the king of Israel the words that you speak in your bedroom." So he said, "Go and see where he is, so that I may send [men] and seize him." And he was told, "He is in Dothan." So he sent horses and chariots and a powerful army there. They came by night and surrounded the city.
>
> —2 KINGS 6:8–14

The prophet Elisha was warning the king of Israel what the king of Aram was plotting in his bedroom; Elisha was revealing the king's plan to make war against Israel. The warning Elisha gave to the king of Israel was so accurate that the king of Aram thought he had a spy among his own ranks who was helping Israel! As the plans of the king of Aram were being set in motion behind closed doors, Elisha the prophet was revealing and exposing those plans to the king of Israel before they could even happen.

This has not changed in the modern day. The call and the office of prophet have not changed. Though our world has changed, technology has advanced, and wickedness has increased throughout the earth, prophets today are still meant to announce the plans of almighty God and what is to come. We are also meant to expose the darkness and shine a spotlight by the revelation that God gives us about the plans of the enemy so that, through the intercession of the people of God and through Christ Jesus, the plans of the kingdom of darkness can be thwarted, dismantled, and cast down.

Prophets, as part of the fivefold ministry, are intended as

well to stand in the gap, exposing the plans of the enemy and holding them off so the rest of the fivefold ministers—the pastors, the teachers, the evangelists, and the apostles—can do their jobs in the kingdom of God!

> In conclusion, be strong in the Lord [draw your strength from Him and be empowered through your union with Him] and in the power of His [boundless] might. Put on the full armor of God [for His precepts are like the splendid armor of a heavily-armed soldier], so that you may be able to [successfully] stand up against all the schemes and the strategies and the deceits of the devil. For our struggle is not against flesh and blood [contending only with physical opponents], but against the rulers, against the powers, against the world forces of this [present] darkness, against the spiritual forces of wickedness in the heavenly (supernatural) places.
>
> —EPHESIANS 6:10–12

CHAPTER 2

WHAT IS TRUTH?

W HAT IS TRUTH? That is a question Pontius Pilate
asked when Jesus was brought to him before the
crucifixion, and it is a question people have continued to ask through the ages. And in this day and
age of social media, artificial intelligence (AI), fake news,
political correctness, and so forth, it has become a loaded
question.

THE WORD OF GOD IS THE TRUTH

There are some definitions of *truth* that are worth exam-
ining. *Merriam-Webster* defines *truth* as "the body of real
things, events, and facts, actuality; the state of being the case,
fact; a transcendent fundamental or spiritual reality; a judgment, proposition, or idea that is true or accepted as true;
the property (as of a statement) of being in accord with fact
or reality."[1] *Collins English Dictionary* says, "The truth about
something is all the facts about it, rather than things that are
imagined or invented."[2]

The Bible has much to say about truth. It says God is
abounding in truth (Exod. 34:6) and that He is "a God of
truth" (Deut. 32:4, NKJV). We are told to serve the Lord "in
sincerity and in truth" (Josh. 24:14). Psalm 40:11 says, "Do

not withhold Your compassion and tender mercy from me, O LORD; Your lovingkindness and Your truth will continually preserve me." The Bible also tells us that God desires truth to be in our innermost beings (Ps. 51:6), and it says, "The truth will set you free [from the penalty of sin]" (John 8:32).

Baker's *Evangelical Dictionary of Biblical Theology* says, "In Scripture, truth is characterized by both qualitative and quantitative aspects. In the historical narratives of the Old Testament, truth is identified with personal veracity and historical factuality."[3] An example of this is in Genesis 42, which states that Joseph put his brothers in prison when they went to Egypt to find food during the famine. He recognized his brothers, but his brothers did not recognize him. He told them, "You shall be kept in prison, that your words may be tested to see whether there is any truth in you" (v. 16, NKJV). Joseph wanted to test them to see if there was truth in them. And when he overheard their confession—a confession that they were guilty of sinning against Joseph when they threw him in the well and then sold him into slavery—Joseph recognized the truth was in them. What they said demonstrated both "personal veracity and historical factuality."

The Bible is the ultimate source of truth. It is the written Word of God, and we know that Jesus is the Word of God made flesh (John 1:14) and that He said, "I am the way, the truth, and the life" (John 14:6, NKJV). Psalm 119:160 says, "The entirety of Your word is truth" (NKJV).

Oswald Chambers says in *Devotions for a Deeper Life*, "The Bible is a universe of revelation facts, not known to unregenerated common sense, and the only exegete of these words is the Holy Spirit."[4] The Holy Spirit, the Ruach HaKodesh, is the Spirit of truth. Truth, by its own nature, will expose lies.

Chambers goes on to say,

Understanding comes only to the degree of the individual's reception, recognition, and reliance on the Holy Spirit. Just as facts in the natural would have to be accepted, so facts in the biblical world of God's will have to be accepted. Our explanation of the facts may be more or less open to dispute. But we can never alter the facts. The Bible is God's revelation of Himself in the interest of grace. Only as we are the recipients of the grace of God will the Bible be opened for us. This Bible is not a book containing communications about God; it is God's giving of himself, in the limitation of words, in the interests of grace. The Bible is not a fairy tale to beguile us for a few moments from the sordid realities of life in the natural world. It is the divine complement of the laws of nature, conscience, and humanity.[5]

Truth is also a standard that measures prophecy and words from the Lord. First Kings 17 tells of when the prophet Elijah interceded for the son of the widow of Zarephath. Her son had just died, and the Lord brought the boy back to life. When Elijah returned the boy to the arms of his mother and said, "See, your son is alive," the widow responded, "Now I know that you are a man of God and that the word of the LORD in your mouth is truth" (vv. 23–24). The widow knew it was truth because what was spoken from the Lord through Elijah was upheld.

It is important that prophets speak nothing but truth in the name of the Lord. In 1 Kings 22 when Ahab the king of Israel asked Jehoshaphat the king of Judah to go to battle with him against Aram, Jehoshaphat said they needed to inquire for the word of the Lord first. All four hundred of Ahab's prophets said they would be successful in battle. But Jehoshaphat must have sensed that truth was not in those prophets' mouths, for he asked if there was another prophet they could question. There was one more prophet, Micaiah, but King Ahab said he hated him "because he never prophesies good news for me, but only evil" (v. 8). But Micaiah was a prophet who was willing to speak the truth, even to the king and even when the truth hurt. The prophet Micaiah was summoned, and his first response about whether they should go to battle was both affirmative and sarcastic because everyone in Ahab's company of false prophets was predicting a favorable outcome in battle. But Ahab knew Micaiah was a true prophet, so he got angry and said, "How many times must I make you swear to tell me nothing but the truth in the name of the LORD?" (v. 16). Even a king who surrounded himself with false prophets wanted to make sure he heard truth from the mouth of a true prophet of the Lord.

MIXING TRUTH AND LIES

You must know the truth to recognize what is false. One of the enemy's tactics is to mix truth and lies. False prophets do this often, which is why it is so important to be firmly grounded in the truth.

If we go back to the beginning, to the tree of the knowledge of good and evil in the Garden of Eden, we see the enemy took a little bit of truth and diluted it with a whole lot of lie so that the truth would become more blurred and less clear. This mix of truth and lies provided favorable conditions for the enemy to operate. Man accepted the whole lot of lie because the little bit of truth was falsely validating it.

> Now the serpent was more crafty (subtle, skilled in deceit) than any living creature of the field which the LORD God had made. And the serpent (Satan) said to the woman, "Can it really be that God has said, 'You

shall not eat from any tree of the garden'?" And the woman said to the serpent, "We may eat fruit from the trees of the garden, except the fruit from the tree which is in the middle of the garden. God said, 'You shall not eat from it nor touch it, otherwise you will die.'" But the serpent said to the woman, "You certainly will not die! For God knows that on the day you eat from it your eyes will be opened [that is, you will have greater awareness], and you will be like God, knowing [the difference between] good and evil."

—Genesis 3:1–5

The truth in his statement was, "Your eyes will be opened [that is, you will have greater awareness]." The lie of the enemy was, "You certainly will not die!" The enemy loves to remove consequences from an action to deceive you into believing that action will not hurt or harm.

First, the enemy craftily got Eve to dismiss the consequences that the Lord Himself put in place for eating of that tree, and then he enticed her by telling her the truth without telling her the whole truth of the massive ripple effect that her and Adam's disobedience would cause through time and history.

Don't fall into the same trap. Don't let a little bit of truth cause you to believe a whole lot of lie.

My Truth?

There is a battle over truth that has increased in intensity every decade up to the current day. The key question of this chapter—What is truth?—is becoming more and more relevant.

In today's world you hear a lot of people say, "Well, this is *my* truth." Well, here's the truth about that: Just because it's your truth doesn't mean it's actually truth. One can say, "My truth is that the sky is purple and the grass is orange," but that doesn't mean it's the truth. In fact, that is not truth. When we look at the sky and the grass, when we look at the evidence, we see the sky is blue and the grass is green—and that is truth. One might say, "My truth is that my life has no purpose, so I may as well give up," but that is not the truth. The truth is that you are God's masterpiece; that you are fearfully and wonderfully made; that God has good plans for you, plans to give you hope and a future; and that God has called you according to His purpose and is working all things for your good (Eph. 2:10; Ps. 139:14; Jer. 29:11; Rom. 8:28).

The phrase *my truth* means that truth is relative, that there is no absolute truth about anything—and that in itself is a lie being perpetrated by the kingdom of darkness. Satan is the father of lies (John 8:44). While there are times when what someone claims as "my truth" is the truth, many times it is a deception, a lie masquerading as the truth. Satan uses the lies behind *my truth* to steal, kill, and destroy the truth and the seeds of faith taking root in your heart, as well as your purpose, your calling, your faith, your freedom, and many other things. That is why it is so important to have a solid understanding of what truth really is. If you don't know the truth, you can be easily deceived by the lies of the enemy.

WITNESSES AND WATCHMEN

In courts of law there is an oath that court officers ask every individual taking the stand: "Do you solemnly swear to tell the truth, the whole truth, and nothing but the truth, so help you God?" Truthful testimony is so vital that oaths for witnesses have been used for centuries in countries all over the world. Proverbs 14:25 says, "A truthful witness saves lives, but he who speaks lies is treacherous."

Truthful witnesses are what we are to be as believers living in a world saturated by corruption, deception, and fabrication.

What is a witness? *Merriam-Webster* defines a *witness* as "one that gives evidence; *specifically*: one who testifies in a cause or before a judicial tribunal...one who has personal knowledge of something; something serving as evidence or proof."[6] A witness is someone who validates a claim. A witness validates and ratifies the order and details of events that have taken place.

The Word of God and the testimony of its writers witness that Jesus Christ came to the earth as the Passover Lamb and willingly purchased us on the cross with the highest price; He paid for the greatest debt in history—the sins of humanity. As believers we are witnesses for Christ. We have personal knowledge of Him, and we serve as living proof of His power, love, mercy, and grace. Our lives should be validators of the claim that the Word of God is true, living, active, and transformative. As witnesses, we testify of the good news that Jesus died and rose again!

Ephesians 6:14 says, "So stand firm and hold your ground, having tightened the wide band of truth (personal integrity, moral courage) around your waist and having put on the breastplate of righteousness (an upright heart)." This verse is part of the apostle Paul's description of the armor of God. The belt, or *wide band* in this translation, is meant to hold armor steady and in place and to keep the armor from falling. A belt is also utilized to hold weapons in place.

Paul told us to tighten the belt of truth. To *tighten* means to draw something closer, to make it fit close to the body, to make it strongly fixed and secure. To draw truth closer to you, you tighten your ranks of beliefs and hold truth close to your life. When Jesus was praying for us before His arrest, He said, "Your word is truth" (John 17:17). The Word of God is the truth that we need to draw close to us. The Word of

God is the truth that we need to make strongly fixed and secure in our hearts and minds.

There are many out there today with bullhorns of bravado and areas of influence that have become the mouthpieces of the serpent on a mass scale. They twist the truth by asking, "Did God really say...?" or, "Did God really mean...?" They begin to speak the adulterated truth of the serpent, the little bit of truth mixed with a whole lot of lie. It is an alternative truth—*their* truth—but it has no alignment with the Word of God. It is not the truth. It is an attempt to taint and manipulate the Word of God, just as the serpent did in the Garden of Eden in Genesis and just as Satan did when he tempted Jesus in the wilderness in Matthew 4.

The prophets of Baal and Asherah (also known as Ashtoreth) on many occasions attempted to speak an alternative truth that had no business with the things of God. They even prophesied. Four hundred fifty prophets of Baal and four hundred prophets of Asherah attempted on a broad scale to make Israel believe and align with a lie that was parading itself as truth. Through their lies, the false prophets were trying to make the people believe that Baal, rather than the Lord, was God. But that lie masquerading as the truth was tested on Mount Carmel. The prophet Elijah confronted the people of Israel, saying, "How long will you hesitate between two opinions? If the LORD is God, follow Him; but if Baal, follow him" (1 Kings 18:21; see also vv. 17–20).

As a prophet, Elijah had the mantle to call the people to repentance and remind them of what the truth really was. He proposed a contest to see whether Baal or Jehovah was the one true God. Elijah declared that the deity who burned up the sacrifice first would be the true God, so he called down fire from heaven—and the truth won. (See 1 Kings 18:22–38.) He announced, "O LORD, the God of Abraham,

Isaac, and Israel (Jacob), let it be known today that You are God in Israel and that I am Your servant and that I have done all these things at Your word. Answer me, O LORD, answer me, so that this people may know that You, O LORD, are God, and that You have turned their hearts back [to You]" (vv. 36–37). Then fire came down from heaven in front of all Israel and consumed the sacrifice, and the people of Israel fell on their faces and proclaimed, "The LORD, He is God! The LORD, He is God!" (v. 39).

This cycle has repeated through the ages, as the enemy thrives in cycles. False prophets appear, claiming to be speaking truth while they lead people away from the Lord. The people are deceived and fall away—unless there is someone who points them back to almighty God.

For example, when the World Economic Forum (WEF) was created in 1971, the first meeting attracted 450 people from dozens of countries. Just as there were 450 people at the first meeting, there were 450 prophets of Baal to face off against the prophet Elijah on Mount Carmel. The enemy cannot create; he can only manipulate what already exists. This is why he works in cycles, and you will see numbers, events, and circumstances continue in cycles as the enemy attempts to gain an edge through them.

This means as believers we need to be watchmen on the wall. Watchmen speak the truth of what they see approaching and sound the alarm for what others cannot see. With the Spirit of truth, watchmen expose the plots and plans of the approaching enemy.

Isaiah 62:6 says, "On your walls, O Jerusalem, I have appointed and stationed watchmen (prophets), who will never keep silent day or night." Jeremiah 6:17 says, "I have set watchmen (prophets) over you, saying, 'Listen and pay attention to the [warning] sound of the trumpet!'" During biblical times watchmen were positioned high on the walls of a city or even in watchtowers so coming threats were easier to spot. The watchmen were responsible for guarding cities. They protected the cities and the people from surprise attacks from enemies and other threats. If they saw something or someone dangerous approaching, they sounded the alarm and warned the people so they could get to safety and prepare to defend against any attacks.

The Hebrew word for *watchman* is *šāmar*. It means to hedge about, to guard, to protect, to take heed, to keep, to watch for, to preserve, and to beware.[7] The Bible also refers to and characterizes watchmen in a spiritual sense. It says that God appointed prophets as spiritual watchmen over the souls of His people; prophets were also watchmen over the soul of a nation and the leadership of that nation.

> Son of man, I have made you a watchman for the people of Israel; so hear the word I speak and give them warning from me.
>
> —EZEKIEL 33:7, NIV

> The watchman of Ephraim is with my God; but the prophet is a fowler's snare in all his ways—enmity in the house of his God.
>
> —HOSEA 9:8, NKJV

> For thus the Lord says to me, "Go, station the lookout, let him report what he sees."
>
> —ISAIAH 21:6, NASB

The Bible says to speak the truth in love (Eph. 4:15). Well, love has many faces, and truth is not always popular. In fact, when a prophet is speaking truth against the lies of the enemy, it creates a rage in those who are peddlers of dressed-up lies.

But the truth still needs to be spoken in love. That is what prophets are called to do.

In the revelationary war that rages on today, the shepherds of the flock shy away from speaking truth because it affects their bottom line. This is part of the reason our nation has been ravaged over the years by doctrines of devils and evil alternative agendas that are meant to lull believers to sleep or draw them further and further away from the truth. The alternative to the truth has been very enticing. It encourages people to stay comfortable in their sin. The enemy will make people feel nice and comfortable in a prison of lies so he can feed their flesh and prevent them from hearing truth, receiving the truth, and being set free. "The truth will set you free" (John 8:32)—not *my truth*, not a little bit of truth with a whole lot of lie mixed in, and not the outright lies of the enemy. It is truth that leads the jail cell to be unlocked and people to experience true freedom through Christ.

The enemy has been spreading the doctrines of devils and evil alternative agendas on a mass scale in our nation and around the world.

> Let no one in any way deceive or entrap you, for that day will not come unless the apostasy comes first [that is, the great rebellion, the abandonment of the faith by professed Christians], and the man of lawlessness is revealed, the son of destruction [the Antichrist, the one who is destined to be destroyed], who opposes and exalts himself [so proudly and so insolently] above every so-called god or object of worship, so that he [actually enters and] takes his seat in the temple of God, publicly proclaiming that he himself is God. Do you not remember that when I was still with you, I was telling you these things? And you know what restrains him now [from being revealed];

it is so that he will be revealed at his own [appointed] time. For the mystery of lawlessness [rebellion against divine authority and the coming reign of lawlessness] is already at work; [but it is restrained] only until he who now restrains it is taken out of the way. Then the lawless one [the Antichrist] will be revealed and the Lord Jesus will slay him with the breath of His mouth and bring him to an end by the appearance of His coming. The coming of the [Antichrist, the lawless] one is through the activity of Satan, [attended] with great power [all kinds of counterfeit miracles] and [deceptive] signs and false wonders [all of them lies], and by unlimited seduction to evil and with all the deception of wickedness for those who are perishing, because they did not welcome the love of the truth [of the gospel] so as to be saved [they were spiritually blind, and rejected the truth that would have saved them]. Because of this God will send upon them a misleading influence, [an activity of error and deception] so they will believe the lie, in order that all may be judged and condemned who did not believe the truth [about their sin, and the need for salvation through Christ], but instead took pleasure in unrighteousness.

—2 THESSALONIANS 2:3–12

We are living in the times described by the apostle Paul in his second letter to the Thessalonians. Lawlessness, destruction, rebellion, abandonment of faith, apostasy, deception, spiritual blindness, pleasure in the unrighteous—these are all terms that describe the world we are living in. That is why believers must be firmly grounded in the truth. Romans 12:2 says,

> And do not be conformed to this world [any longer with its superficial values and customs], but be transformed and progressively changed [as you mature spiritually] by the renewing of your mind [focusing on godly values and ethical attitudes], so that you may prove [for yourselves] what the will of God is, that which is good and acceptable and perfect [in His plan and purpose for you].

How do you renew your mind? With the Word of God. His Word is truth.

You need the Word in your mind, but you also need it in your heart. Psalm 119:11 says, "Your word I have treasured and stored in my heart." Deuteronomy 11:18–21 (NKJV) says,

> Therefore you shall lay up these words of mine in your heart and in your soul....You shall teach them to your children, speaking of them when you sit in your house, when you walk by the way, when you lie down, and when you rise up. And you shall write them on the doorposts of your house and on your gates, that your days and the days of your children may be multiplied.

There is peace in the Word. There is protection in the Word. We must have the Word in our hearts and minds.

The world we live in is a scary place these days, and it seems as if it gets worse every day. But God has not given you a spirit of fear (2 Tim. 1:7). Oswald Chambers writes, "The remarkable thing about fearing God is that when you fear God you fear nothing else, whereas if you do not fear God you fear everything else."[8]

During this revelationary war, you do not need to fear the enemy. Fear God. Look to Jesus. Cling to the truth. Get it in your mind and in your heart. When the prophets speak, "pay attention and weigh carefully what is said" (1 Cor. 14:29). Remember that you must know the truth to recognize what is false. And let "the peace of God, which surpasses all understanding…guard your hearts and minds through Christ Jesus" (Phil. 4:7, NKJV).

CHAPTER 3

BACK TO THE GARDEN: "DID GOD REALLY SAY...?"

"IN THE BEGINNING God (Elohim) created [by forming from nothing] the heavens and the earth" (Gen. 1:1). The Lord made earth as a place for man to dwell with Him in communion. God created the earth as a place where man would be given dominion to rule over it and all the living creatures within it. This is the revelation of God's order with man:

> Then God said, "Let Us (Father, Son, Holy Spirit) make man in Our image, according to Our likeness [not physical, but a spiritual personality and moral likeness]; and let them have complete authority over the fish of the sea, the birds of the air, the cattle, and over the entire earth, and over everything that creeps and crawls on the earth." So God created man in His own image, in the image and likeness of God He created him; male and female He created them. And God blessed them [granting them certain authority] and said to them, "Be fruitful, multiply, and fill the earth, and subjugate it [putting it under your power]; and rule over (dominate) the fish of the

sea, the birds of the air, and every living thing that
moves upon the earth."

—GENESIS 1:26–28

And God saw that it was good (v. 31).

However, there is an entity that does not see God's creation as good. There is an entity that does not see the creation of man's dominion on the earth as good. There is an entity that wants full control over the heavens and the earth and all that is in them. There is an entity that led a full-on rebellion in the heavenlies to attempt to usurp the throne of almighty God, Elohim.

That entity is Satan.

Remember, Satan is the father of lies. The origin of lies is rooted in the actions he took because he did not want to share any of what God had given him when he was a high-ranking angel. Then, at the dawn of creation, as described in Genesis 1, he saw before him God's incredible ability to create. And not only did God have an amazing ability to create, but He also created man in His own image. But the image of God was an image Satan was desperate to corrupt and tarnish. Out of this rebellion and desperation, a plan was developed and executed to corrupt the entire earth and to tarnish and ruin what the Lord had created and called good.

The revelationary war's first attack was launched at a tree, a very special tree in the middle of a perfect garden. This was the opening attack of Satan's "Did God really say...?" tactic (Gen. 3:1, NIV). It was the attack intended to cause man to doubt a perfect God's perfect will for man in a whole and untarnished earth. This is also when the first tiny seeds of wokeism were put in the earth to be activated and grown within a window of history. We will explore that in a later chapter.

When mankind fell, all that was created with it fell as

well. It was a cataclysmal blow to all creation and to the Lord's heart, which would be grieved beyond what we can comprehend and by more than the decisions we are about to examine.

THE TREE OF THE KNOWLEDGE OF GOOD AND EVIL

When the Lord created man and placed him in the Garden of Eden, He gave man free will. That is why the tree of the knowledge of good and evil was placed in the center of the garden, in the heart of the garden. The choice to obey God was a choice of man's heart. The Lord wanted man to choose Him every day over any desires to partake of that tree. Almighty God, Adam and Eve's Creator and Father, wanted their desires to love and serve and *obey* Him to be far greater than the desire to disobey the law of the garden. For God is the law and the Word.

> In the beginning [before all time] was the Word (Christ), and the Word was with God, and the Word was God Himself. He was [continually existing] in the beginning [co-eternally] with God. All things were made and came into existence through Him; and without Him not even one thing was made that has come into being. In Him was life [and the power to bestow life], and the life was the Light of men. The Light shines on in the darkness, and the darkness did not understand it or overpower it or appropriate it or absorb it [and is unreceptive to it].
>
> —JOHN 1:1–5

So man was placed in a beautiful garden to cultivate and tend it, and it was a place where man could walk and talk with God. Enter the serpent, the vehicle of a false revelation to be presented to man. Again, here's Eve's encounter with the serpent:

> Now the serpent was more crafty (subtle, skilled in deceit) than any living creature of the field which the LORD God had made. And the serpent (Satan) said to the woman, "Can it really be that God has said, 'You shall not eat from any tree of the garden'?" And the woman said to the serpent, "We may eat fruit from the trees of the garden, except the fruit from the tree which is in the middle of the garden. God said, 'You shall not eat from it nor touch it, otherwise you will die.'"
>
> —GENESIS 3:1–3

The first shots were fired with a question: "Can it really be that God has said...?" This was when doubt entered the earth and the garden. The fleshly pull of doubt began to tug at Eve as Satan started the revelationary war.

The word for *serpent* in Hebrew is *nachash* (or *nāḥaš*). The root word of *nachash* means to hiss, but it has other meanings, including to whisper a spell, to use enchantment, to practice divination or fortune-telling, and to take as an omen.[1] There is a clear connection between *nachash*, or *serpent*, and supernatural forces; that is, the supernatural forces of the kingdom of darkness.

First Samuel 15:23 says, "For rebellion is as the sin of witchcraft" (NKJV). For rebellion to occur, the *nachash*, the serpent, is present in some form to whisper his spell of lies. In the Garden of Eden the serpent deceived the woman by spelling out in a different way what the Lord already clearly said.

> But the serpent said to the woman, "You certainly will not die! For God knows that on the day you eat from it

your eyes will be opened [that is, you will have greater awareness], and you will be like God, knowing [the difference between] good and evil." And when the woman saw that the tree was good for food, and that it was delightful to look at, and a tree to be desired in order to make one wise and insightful, she took some of its fruit and ate it; and she also gave some to her husband with her, and he ate. Then the eyes of the two of them were opened [that is, their awareness increased], and they knew that they were naked; and they fastened fig leaves together and made themselves coverings.

—GENESIS 3:4–7

The enemy sowed doubt first, and then he came in with the great deception: "You certainly will not die!" The serpent's lie, his whispered spell of deceit, was in direct opposition to the instructions given by the Lord and the consequences the Lord laid out for disobeying the law of the Garden of Eden.

The serpent followed up the deception with sowing rebellion, encouraging them to rebel against the laws of God. He targeted Eve to get her to believe that the Lord was trying to keep them from realizing their full potential and becoming similar to Him. The enemy knew good and well the wage for rebellion and sin—he paid it when he launched his full-on rebellion against the Lord in the heavenlies. He fell from heaven and was eternally separated from fellowship with God. He knew that a fall would be the result for a rebellious man too. And he knew no one is like almighty God. He was basically saying, "You do not need to be beneath the Lord and follow His law. You can be His equal and know all that He does." Today, he might have phrased it, "You can be woke."

The serpent knew the way to get to Adam was Eve. To corrupt someone that Adam deeply loved would emotionally pull Adam in with her. That is why Eve was the serpent's first target.

Notice when the serpent said, "Did God really say...?" Eve's response wasn't what God really said. God said, in essence, "Don't eat," but Eve essentially said, "God said, 'Don't eat or touch'" (Gen. 2:17; 3:3). When the enemy comes with deception, we must be on guard. Eve responded with the Word of the Lord, but she added to it. While she could have misunderstood God's command or remembered it wrong, her addition also could have been a step on the road to legalism. It is never good to add things that God didn't really say to what He's said. Satan likes to twist the Word of God; don't help him. When the enemy targets you with deception, "stand your ground, putting on the belt of truth" (Eph. 6:14, NLT).

Once the fruit was eaten and the law of God was violated, there was a cataclysmal change in the earth. The enemy had deceived man into giving up the dominion over the earth that was given by God, now giving the enemy the upper hand. However, the Lord, knowing that man had been given free will and knowing what that could cause, had a contingency plan for this. God's plan was activated the moment Adam partook of the fruit. Jesus Christ, Son of God Most High, would be birthed into the earth at the appointed time, and He would die for the sins of humanity so humanity could take back dominion of the earth.

DEFLECTION

The exchange between the Lord, Adam, Eve, and the serpent is one that would echo throughout history.

> Then the eyes of the two of them were opened [that is, their awareness increased], and they knew that they

were naked; and they fastened fig leaves together and made themselves coverings.

And they heard the sound of the LORD God walking in the garden in the cool [afternoon breeze] of the day, so the man and his wife hid and kept themselves hidden from the presence of the LORD God among the trees of the garden. But the LORD God called to Adam, and said to him, "Where are you?" He said, "I heard the sound of You [walking] in the garden, and I was afraid because I was naked; so I hid myself." God said, "Who told you that you were naked? Have you eaten [fruit] from the tree of which I commanded you not to eat?" And the man said, "The woman whom You gave to be with me— she gave me [fruit] from the tree, and I ate it." Then the LORD God said to the woman, "What is this that you have done?" And the woman said, "The serpent beguiled and deceived me, and I ate [from the forbidden tree]."

—GENESIS 3:7–13

The war of deflection that dominates the media and political arena today began in the Garden of Eden. What does it mean to deflect? According to *Cambridge Dictionary*, *deflection* means "the act of attacking or blaming another person rather than accepting criticism or blame for your own actions."[2] This has saturated the political arena and the media, and now it has even infiltrated the church.

When the Lord began to question Adam and Eve, He questioned Adam first because he was supposed to be the head. Adam, in that moment, did not accept responsibility for what he did and ask for forgiveness and mercy from the Lord. Instead, he said, "The woman whom You gave to be with me—she gave me [fruit] from the tree, and I ate it." Adam was basically saying, "You are at fault here, God, because You gave me this woman who now has taken me down with her."

Then the Lord turned to Eve: "What is this that you have done?"

Eve deflected as well: "The serpent deceived me, and I ate" (NKJV). Here, Eve was saying, "God, it's all the serpent's fault."

Each one deflected the responsibility for their disobedience onto someone else. They refused accountability for their actions, for their disobedience to the Lord in partaking of the one tree, the tree of the knowledge of good and evil, that the Lord strictly told them not to. The voice of the serpent became louder and more influential than the voice of the Lord in that moment.

The enemy must always get you to doubt a belief or conviction before he can get you to change your direction. Again, that is why you must be firmly grounded in the truth of the Word. When you know the truth, it is easier to recognize the lie of the enemy.

And if the enemy does succeed in getting you to change your direction, if he succeeds in getting you to give in to temptation, don't deflect. Take responsibility for your actions. Repent. Get back to right relationship with the Lord. Accept His forgiveness, His mercy, and His grace. Make sure that belt of truth is buckled firmly around your waist. Make it harder for the enemy's lies and deception to drown out the voice of the Lord in your life.

CONSEQUENCES

Because of the life-changing meal at the tree in the heart of the Garden of Eden, the serpent was cursed more than all the cattle and made to slither on its belly. Enmity was put between the woman and the serpent. It is a sobering warning to us all—be careful who sits at your table, and be very careful what kind of meal you consume.

When the Lord cursed the serpent, He said,

> And I will put enmity (open hostility) between you and the woman, and between your seed (offspring) and her Seed; He shall [fatally] bruise your head, and you shall [only] bruise His heel.
>
> —GENESIS 3:15

This verse put God's contingency plan in motion—the plan for Jesus Christ to be birthed into the earth. The Word became flesh and crushed the head of Satan by willingly dying at Calvary, purchasing us sinners by His own blood. He defeated hell, death, and the grave by rising from the dead on the third day. After His resurrection, He even appeared to many people over a forty-day period, continuing to teach the disciples and reveal the truth of His Word. This whole plan was put into motion when the Lord cursed the serpent in the Garden of Eden.

The Lord then spoke to the woman. Because of her disobedience, pain in childbirth was greatly multiplied. All the women of the earth have Eve to thank for that. I think this is why God allowed the invention of epidurals! The Lord also told Eve that Adam would rule over her and be responsible for her because of her lapse in judgment. (See Genesis 3:16.)

Adam's turn was next.

> Then to Adam the LORD God said, "Because you have listened [attentively] to the voice of your wife, and have eaten [fruit] from the tree about which I commanded you, saying, 'You shall not eat of it'; the ground is [now] under a curse because of you; in sorrow and toil you shall eat [the fruit] of it all the days of your life. Both

> thorns and thistles it shall grow for you; and you shall
> eat the plants of the field."
>
> —GENESIS 3:17–18

There were no weeds in the earth until this was spoken. No such invasive plants that harmed vegetation existed. The introduction of sin into the earth went even into the soil, and from that point on, every edible plant and tree would have to fight to grow and stretch out its roots for the precious water and resources that weeds steal.

Weeds will steal resources. They steal, kill, and destroy what God created to be good. That is why even today we must weed our gardens; otherwise, growth and bearing good fruit are severely hampered. This applies to our lives and our souls as well. If we don't weed, root out, and tear up the invasive things the enemy puts in our lives to steal, kill, and destroy, those weeds will take over and devastate the fruit we are meant to bear as children of God Most High.

When this shot of deception, this shot of "Did God really say…?" was fired that day in the garden, it was truly the shot across the bow that began the revelationary war, a war that has continued to be fought through the generations. It is a war of influence, a war of deflection, and a war meant to replace the truth and instructions of God—which are just, are right, and bear much fruit—with the doctrines of demons in the lives of humanity. Replacement theology began in the garden. And since that day, Satan has fervently desired to replace the life-giving theology of God and His kingdom with a theology of darkness that stunts growth, deceives, and invades all areas of life. Satan comes to steal, kill, and destroy (John 10:10). His theology of darkness is meant to fracture the relationship between man and the Lord and to cause God's own creation to oppose Him. The revelationary war that began in the garden is having a serious effect in our modern day. The war is raging.

It is a war with false prophecy parading itself as the truth from God. The true voices of the servants of God Most High are battling the false prophets that have inserted themselves into media, the church, and the political arena. It really is a war of revelation. This war has reached a fever pitch in our time, and there is a call to the people of God to truly get into His Word and discern who the real enemy is. We are about to embark on a journey to examine what caused this war to escalate to a historic level in our present day.

CHAPTER 4

THE JEHOSHAPHAT– AHAB PARADIGM: THE PROPHECY MATRIX

N CHAPTER 2 we looked at the time when King Ahab asked King Jehoshaphat to go into battle with him. In the account we see four separate entities came together, and a battle of revelation ensued. What happened, as told in that chapter of the Bible, can very much be applied to what we see transpiring today.

First, there was Jehoshaphat, the king of Judah. He was a godly king who followed in the ways of the Lord. He sought out the truth of the Lord and made important decisions based on it.

Next, there was Ahab, the king of Israel. Ahab and Jehoshaphat were related by marriage.

Ahab was a rebellious king who married Jezebel, high priestess of Baal, for political purposes, and together Ahab and Jezebel led Israel into the idolatrous worship of false gods. This caused them to break covenant with almighty God. An Ahab will almost always drag people with good intentions into their transgressions.

Then there were also the four hundred "prophets" that Ahab called and assembled to inquire about whether the armies of Israel and Judah would be victorious in battle. This group of false prophets was being controlled by the regime of Ahab and Jezebel.

Lastly, there was Micaiah, a true servant of God and prophet of the Lord.

These were the four main entities that came together in a clash—a historic clash.

SHALL WE GO TO WAR?

While the story of Ahab, Jehoshaphat, Micaiah, and the false prophets is found in 1 Kings 22, it is also found in 2 Chronicles 18. In the Jewish culture the number eighteen stands for life. It is very significant that this account is in chapter 18 of 2 Chronicles because Ahab's life especially hangs in the balance before God's throne.

The eighteenth letter of the Hebrew alphabet is *tzaddik*. According to Rabbi Aaron Raskin,

> The name *tzaddik* means "righteous one," a leader and teacher of a generation. We also know that many *tzaddikim* are called rebbe. This tradition began with Moses, the first rebbe of the Jewish people....There is a rebbe in every generation, a *tzaddik* who is that era's spiritual leader...."Rebbe"...is an acronym for *Rosh B'nei Yisrael*, "the head of the Jewish people."[1]

Micaiah could be viewed as one of these *tzaddikim*, or righteous ones. He was a true prophet in a time when many in Israel and Judah had turned to false gods, and as such he served as a spiritual leader. In the natural, Micaiah was outnumbered by four hundred rogue prophets and one very rebellious king, but he remained faithful to his prophetic calling.

The story began,

> Ahab king of Israel said to Jehoshaphat king of Judah, "Will you go with me to [fight against] Ramoth-gilead?" He answered, "I am as you are, and my people as your people [your hopes and concerns are ours]; we will be with you in the battle."
>
> Further, Jehoshaphat said to the king of Israel, "Please inquire first for the word of the LORD." Then the king of Israel assembled the prophets, four hundred men, and said to them, "Shall we go against Ramoth-gilead to battle, or shall I refrain?" And they said, "Go up, for God will hand it over to the king." But Jehoshaphat said, "Is there no prophet of the LORD still here by whom we may inquire?" The king of Israel said to Jehoshaphat, "There is still one man by whom we may inquire of the LORD, but I hate him, for he never prophesies [anything] good for me, but always evil. He is Micaiah the son of Imla." And Jehoshaphat said, "Let not the king say so [perhaps this time it will be different]."
>
> —2 CHRONICLES 18:3–7

When Ahab said, "I hate him," about Micaiah, what Ahab really hated was what was *in* Micaiah—the power of God that controls the rise and fall of kings and that can shape nations.

Romans 1:18 says, "For [God does not overlook sin and] the wrath of God is revealed from heaven against all ungodliness and unrighteousness of men who in their wickedness suppress and stifle the truth." A godly leader always concerns himself first with what the Lord has to say concerning a nation. This was the case with Jehoshaphat. Second Chronicles 17:3–4 says,

The LORD was with Jehoshaphat because he followed the example of his father (ancestor) David. He did not seek [to follow] the Baals [the false gods], but sought the God of his father, and walked in (obeyed) His commandments, and did not act as Israel did.

It was Jehoshaphat, not Ahab, who wanted the word of the Lord before going into any battle. Ahab wanted to leapfrog over the Lord, while Jehoshaphat wanted the Lord to set the course they were to take.

Ahab assembled four hundred false prophets who were funded by Ahab and Jezebel's government. They were talking heads, and they always told Ahab exactly what he wanted to hear. This has similarities to the CIA's Operation Mockingbird, which I will talk about later. The prophets were there to fill Ahab with the delicate dainties of deceit that he so feasted upon his entire reign.

How do we know this? Again, 2 Chronicles 18:6–7 says,

> But Jehoshaphat said, "Is there no prophet of the LORD still here by whom we may inquire?" The king of Israel said to Jehoshaphat, "There is still one man by whom we may inquire of the LORD, but I hate him, for he never prophesies [anything] good for me, but always evil. He is Micaiah the son of Imla."

First off, Ahab was a textbook narcissist. He wanted fake news. He wanted the prophets to tell him what he wanted to hear. He did *not* want the truth. The rulers of the darkness of this world lured him to craving the deception over the truth.

The Lord was with Jehoshaphat, so he realized that the prophets were not speaking the truth. So Jehoshaphat was a voice of truth in the midst of the deception, and he outed the four hundred men who were supposed to be godly prophets.

He asked, "Is there no prophet of the LORD still here by whom we may inquire?" In a nutshell Jehoshaphat was saying to Ahab, "All your prophets neither hear from God nor serve Him, and we will not get the truth from them." These so-called prophets were submitted to Baal's system, not God's kingdom. Therefore, how could they ever recognize the voice of the Lord?

HATE SPEECH OR TRUTH?

King Ahab then mentioned Micaiah, a true prophet of the Lord. However, Ahab openly said he hated him because "he never prophesies [anything] good for me, but always evil." Basically, Ahab was saying that with Micaiah there was accountability. Ahab's corruption was called to account. "Micaiah doesn't tell me what I want to hear. He tells me the blatant truth."

Truth will always be hate speech to those who want to believe a lie.

Even though King Ahab hated him for it, Micaiah continued to speak the truth. That was because Micaiah feared God above man. He was more concerned with speaking the truth than with appeasing consciences and tickling the ears of his audience. God's truth carries more weight than man's accolades.

Ahab craved the fake news and not the good news! That means his world was shaped around deceptions, lies, and blasphemous exploits. "The wages of sin is death" (Rom. 6:23). This is very clear in God's Word.

The story continues,

> Then the king of Israel called for an officer and said, "Bring Micaiah the son of Imla quickly." Now the king of Israel and Jehoshaphat the king of Judah were sitting, each on his throne, arrayed in their robes; they

> were sitting at the threshing floor at the entrance of
> the gate of Samaria; and all the prophets were prophe-
> sying before them. Zedekiah the son of Chenaanah had
> made horns of iron for himself; and said, "Thus says
> the LORD: 'With these you shall gore the Arameans
> (Syrians) until they are destroyed.'" All the prophets
> prophesied this, saying, "Go up to Ramoth-gilead and
> succeed; the LORD will hand it over to the king."
>
> —2 CHRONICLES 18:8–11

While Micaiah was being summoned, Ahab's prophets—
the ones who had already sold out to an ungodly regime
—continued to speak forth victory for Ahab at Ramoth-gilead.
Zedekiah made horns of iron; he included these objects in a
false prophecy. Horns were symbols of strength. In a way this
was smoke and mirrors. Zedekiah was utilizing what was tan-
gible to direct Ahab's focus toward him as he put on a grand
show—yes, a show. Ahab's false prophets were showmen,
not shepherds. All four hundred were telling Ahab what he
wanted to hear, that God, whom King Ahab didn't even faithfully serve, was going to give him a great military victory.

These four hundred men were complete strangers to God.
They were ignorant of His ways, and they were deaf to His
voice. However, they presented the illusion of being capable
of accurately bringing forth the word of God.

When the messenger retrieved Micaiah, he actually said
to Micaiah, "'Listen, the words of the prophets are of one
accord, foretelling a favorable outcome for the king. So just
let your word be like one of them and speak favorably.' But
Micaiah said, 'As the LORD lives, I will [only] speak what my
God says'" (vv. 12–13).

Just because a group of people is of one accord does
not mean whatever they are planning is from the Lord. In

Genesis the people were of one accord with Nimrod to build the Tower of Babel and overthrow the Lord, but that doesn't mean it was a wise idea. The Lord intentionally scattered them and caused great confusion so the agreement between them would indeed break. (See Genesis 10:8–10 and 11:1–9.)

The messenger was basically saying, "Tell King Ahab what he wants to hear, Micaiah. Come into line with the majority. Come into agreement with a very large lie so it has the appearance of truth." The enemy often uses this strategy with his deception. The more people who speak the lie, the more the lie appears to be the truth. Micaiah was key to validating a lie for Ahab's administration. That was what Micaiah was being told by the messenger from the king's court—validate the lie.

Micaiah's response was decisive, and it was bold: "As the LORD lives, I will [only] speak what my God says." In a nutshell he was saying, "I am not going to say what you want me to say; I am going to say what the Lord wants me to say, even if it is not popular."

THE FAITHFUL MINORITY

When the prophet Micaiah first arrived in the king's court, he mocked Ahab and said, "Go up and succeed, for they will be handed over to you" (v. 14).

But Ahab realized Micaiah was being sarcastic, and he said, "How many times must I warn you…to tell me nothing but the truth in the name of the LORD?" (v. 15). Ahab was asking for it here. He was almost daring the Lord to defy what his four hundred bought-and-paid-for prophets had said.

> Then Micaiah said, "I saw all [the people of] Israel scattered on the mountains, as sheep that have no shepherd; and the LORD said, 'These have no master. Let each one return to his house in peace.'"

Then the king of Israel said to Jehoshaphat, "Did I not tell you that he would not prophesy good in regard to me, but [only] evil?"

So Micaiah said, "Therefore, hear the word of the LORD: I saw the LORD sitting on His throne, and all the host (army) of heaven standing on His right and on His left. Then the LORD said, 'Who will entice Ahab king of Israel to go up and fall [defeated] at Ramoth-gilead?' And one said this and another said that. Then a spirit came forward and stood before the LORD and said, 'I will entice him.' The LORD said to him, 'By what means?' He said, 'I will go out and be a deceptive spirit in the mouth of all his prophets.' Then the LORD said, 'You are to entice him and also succeed. Go and do so.' Now, you see, the LORD put a deceptive spirit in the mouth of these prophets of yours; and the LORD has [actually] proclaimed disaster against you."

—2 CHRONICLES 18:16–22

Micaiah saw the people of Israel scattered and broken and without a shepherd. Ahab's life was weighing in the balance here, but his response was, "Did I not tell you that he would not prophesy good in regard to me?" Translation: "Micaiah will not tell me what I want to hear or agree with my rebellion."

This was when the revelationary war between the prophets of God and the prophets of Baal reached its crescendo during Ahab's reign. Ahab didn't learn after Elijah-gate on Mount Carmel. Fire came down from heaven, and over eight hundred prophets of Baal and Asherah were executed (1 Kings 18:38–40). You would think that would have shaken Ahab straight. You would think he would have learned his lesson. Instead, Ahab doubled down and continued to push Baal's doctrines out to the people, using the false prophets to make deceptions appear credible. Remember, the enemy will always mix a little bit of truth with a whole lot of lie, and he will have as many people as possible repeat that lie. Don't fall for it, as Ahab did.

It was at this point that Micaiah boldly stood for what the Lord had spoken forth. He was outnumbered in the natural four hundred to one. But here's some truth: You do not need a majority to defeat evil. You need a faithful minority partnering with and submitting to almighty God.

That was exactly what Micaiah did. He was faithful in partnering with and submitting to God. He spoke the word of the Lord—not what Ahab wanted to hear. Micaiah continued and explained the vision God had given him: "I saw the LORD sitting on His throne, and all the host (army) of heaven standing on His right and on His left. Then the LORD said, 'Who will entice Ahab king of Israel to go up and fall [defeated] at Ramoth-gilead?'" (vv. 18–19). Who will lure Ahab to his demise?

The time had come for Ahab to be judged. The grace God had given Ahab had at this point thinned. He and Jezebel, his corrupt wife, had shed much innocent blood, and they had defied the living God by turning the nation of Israel to worship Baal. The charges against Ahab were too great to ignore as the Lord sat on His throne, decisively ruling that Ahab's reign over Israel must come to an end. How was the Lord going to do it? By being wise as a serpent and harmless as a dove and deceiving the deceiver!

Micaiah explained that he saw a spirit step forward and say it would entice Ahab to fall at Ramoth-gilead by going out and being a deceptive spirit in the mouths of Ahab's prophets! This spirit before the throne of God was going to cause Ahab's prophets to prophesy flat-out lies. This would get the king to agree with a lie so he would go out to battle and fall at Ramoth-gilead.

In 2 Chronicles 18:22 Micaiah said, "Now, you see, the LORD put a deceptive spirit in the mouth of these prophets of yours; and the LORD has [actually] proclaimed disaster against you." The very deception that dominated Ahab's rule would be the very thing that now brought about his demise. The very prophets Ahab relied upon to feed his flesh and puff up his ego would be the very people the Lord utilized to lure Ahab to his appointed demise.

> Then Zedekiah the son of Chenaanah came up and struck Micaiah on the cheek and said, "Which way did the Spirit of the LORD go [when he departed] from me to speak to you?" Micaiah said, "Behold, you will see on that day when you go into an inner room [desperately trying] to hide yourself." Then the king of Israel said, "Take Micaiah and return him to Amon the governor of the city and to Joash the king's son, and say, 'Thus says the king: "Put this man in prison and feed him just enough bread and water to survive until I return in peace (safely)."'" But Micaiah said, "If you actually return in peace, the LORD has not spoken by me." And he added, "Listen [to what I have said], you people, all of you."
>
> —2 CHRONICLES 18:23–27

Micaiah was imprisoned because he told the truth and did not come into agreement with the foundation of deception that dominated Ahab's rule as king. Imprisoning Micaiah was Ahab's response to hearing the judgment God intended for him. Imprison the mouthpiece, silence the truth, and run from repentance because the deception sounds more favorable. It happened in Micaiah's day, and it is happening now too.

Through his actions King Ahab chose to continue the delusion he had perpetuated his entire reign. Micaiah's last words to Ahab were, "If you actually return in peace, the LORD has not spoken by me." Then he also said, "Listen [to what I have said], you people, all of you." Hear this day the Word of the Lord, and remember it, for it will accomplish what it has set out to do.

The word of the Lord would certainly not return void (Isa. 55:11); however, the word of the four hundred false prophets would indeed return void because it was empty of any truth.

HIDING NEVER WORKS

Jehoshaphat—even after hearing and seeing all these things—made the decision to go with Ahab into battle, supporting Ahab's delusions, because of their political alliance through marriage. Does this sound familiar? Enabling candidates, parties, or even your family members in the destructive delusions they have defiantly set out to accomplish will always pull you away from the will of God into dangerous territory where you will suffer for your participation in their rebellion and delusions.

> So [Ahab] the king of Israel and Jehoshaphat king of Judah went up against Ramoth-gilead. The king of Israel said to Jehoshaphat, "I will disguise myself and will go into battle, but you put on your [royal] robes." So the king of Israel disguised himself, and they went into the battle.
>
> —2 CHRONICLES 18:28–29

Ahab's solution to almighty God putting a lying spirit in the mouths of his prophets and pronouncing judgment on him was to disguise himself; he believed it would protect him from the judgment being fulfilled. This was a doubling down on deception. His conscience was seared at this point; there was no desire to humble himself before the Lord. Instead, he thought he was going to hide from the Lord and outsmart Him by disguising himself so the opposing army could not find him.

Hiding from the Lord never works. In Genesis, Adam hid from the Lord after he rebelled against the instructions of the Lord (3:8). He was found out and cast out of the garden. Again, "the wages of sin is death" (Rom. 6:23). According to chapter 32 in the Book of Numbers, "Your sin will find you out" (v. 23). There is no place one can run to in order to hide from an ever-present God. There is no deception, trick, or illusion that can be done to hide from His judgments. Thinking he could hide from judgment was pride on Ahab's part. "Pride goes before destruction, and a haughty spirit before a fall" (Prov. 16:18), a big fall in Ahab's case. That lying spirit in the mouths of his prophets caused a haughty spirit in Ahab. His delusion and his desperate desire to prove wrong Micaiah, a true prophet of the Lord, ultimately lured him to his demise.

> Then a certain man drew his bow at random and struck [Ahab] the king of Israel between the scales of his armor. So Ahab said to his chariot driver, "Turn around and take me out of the battle, because I am seriously wounded." The battle raged that day, and the king of Israel propped himself up in his chariot in front of the Arameans (Syrians) until the evening, and at sunset he died.
>
> —2 CHRONICLES 18:33–34

At random. The direction of the man's arrow was not random at all, for the Lord had judged Ahab and determined he was going to die in this particular battle. Neither Jehoshaphat nor Ahab's four hundred prophets nor Ahab's disguising himself to hide his identity could save Ahab from the true word of the Lord that went forth from Micaiah's mouth. The word of the

Lord and Micaiah was upheld, and the four hundred prophets of Ahab were proved to be compromised deceivers who had lost all ability to discern the truth from the lie. The majority was in grave error in this case.

And what happened to Jehoshaphat? Even though Jehoshaphat made a very poor choice to still go into battle with Ahab, and even after hearing the word of the Lord upon his own request, Jehoshaphat was protected by the Lord in battle. However, the Lord chastised Jehoshaphat through a prophet after the battle. (See 2 Chronicles 19:1–3.)

There are those who are authorized by God Himself to speak for God, and then there are those who take it upon themselves to give an illusion that they are qualified and authorized to speak for God when the Lord has not granted them such authorization. They have a spirit of importance, thinking they can speak for God. Through putting on a show or acting as if they are in the know, they create an illusion so they can stand in an office they were never meant to occupy.

Agreement works both ways. Many can agree on a wrong word that attempts to drown out the true word of the Lord. The flesh wants what it wants, and both flesh and access to power can entice one to agree with many things that appear righteous. Inherently, the roots of these things are in darkness, and disaster follows. Again, that is why we must know the truth of God's Word—it enables us to weigh carefully the word being spoken to determine whether it is the truth or just a little bit of truth with a whole lot of lie.

THE WAR RAGES ON

What transpired in the Garden of Eden with Adam, Eve, and the serpent, and what transpired with Jehoshaphat, Micaiah,

Ahab, and the four hundred false prophets have infiltrated humanity and affected our modern-day society.

As I've mentioned, a war of revelation on a scale we have not seen until now has reached a fever pitch in our nation and throughout the earth. This war is raging. True revelation and the Word of God are contending against the vast army of deception, disinformation, propaganda, and false prophets and teachers.

When I was a child, there was a cartoon called *The Transformers*. The transformers have the ability to transform from cars, trucks, and motorcycles into freethinking robots. There is a righteous army and a wicked army. The name of the wicked army is the Decepticons. Their leader seeks to cause chaos and destroy humanity wherever the Decepticons go. The Decepticons find corrupt humans to assist them in their attempt to take over humanity. Satan does the same thing. His army of darkness is much like the Decepticons. His army's goal is to cause chaos and destroy humanity, and it uses deceived humans to help it. This same storyline, of the powers of darkness using deceived and corrupt humans to assist them with their wicked plan, plays out over and over again in movies, TV shows, books, and so forth.

You see, the foundation for what we see happening now was laid long ago. The enemy is using the power of the air and his influence with corrupt figures in business and media to carry out his plan to destroy humanity. The enemy's factions all work together to purposefully cause misdirection, confusion, and outright deception to bring man further away from the Lord, from His covering, and from His truth. The enemy's goal is to get humanity so lost that it cannot find its way back to the Lord.

The enemy will create a multitude of noise in an attempt to drown out the truth of God's Word and what He has to say to His people through His true prophets. The enemy and the kingdom of darkness have more weapons at their disposal in the present day than they have ever had before—television, radio, the music industry, social media, the scientific community (including NASA), megachurches, and digital platforms. Satan utilizes all these avenues. He fashions them as weapons and attacks the minds of believers. He campaigns to cause doubt about God and who He is and what He says, and in doing so, Satan causes the love of many to grow cold.

Ultimately, all this deception and doubt causes the soul to fall into bondage. Once a person's soul is in chains, that person is no longer a threat to Satan and his kingdom of darkness.

The enemy allures you to enslave you. Almighty God allures you to deliver you and set you free through His Son, Jesus Christ.

The enemy comes to steal, kill, and destroy. Jesus Christ came to give life, and life more abundantly (John 10:10).

In the coming chapters we will expose how the enemy has raised up prophets of Baal and Ashtoreth and will expose their strategies and the weapons they have utilized against our generation. Exposing the voices, tactics, and weapons of the deceiver allows us to understand the difference between counterfeit voices and the voice of the Lord through His shepherds, His prophets, and His Word. It allows us to distinguish between the lies and the truth. This is the great generational battle we must win in order for the younger generation to be what the Lord is calling them to be. We are more than conquerors through Christ Jesus (Rom. 8:37), and for the kingdom of God to advance in this time, conquer we must. When the kingdom of God advances in our nation, it will influence other nations in the earth that are on the brink of complete and utter darkness. Armor up according to Ephesians 6 as we go forth, for this battle is the Lord's (1 Sam. 17:47).

THE PROPHECY MATRIX

We are in a time when many who claim to hold the office of a prophet hold no such thing. As I said in chapter 1, there is a significant difference between the gift of prophecy and the office. All those with the indwelling of the Holy Spirit can operate in the gift of prophecy. However, the office is very different. If no such office existed today, Paul would not have written what he did to the Ephesians. Again, he wrote,

> And He Himself gave some to be apostles, some prophets, some evangelists, and some pastors and teachers, for the equipping of the saints for the work of ministry, for the edifying of the body of Christ, till we all come to the unity of the faith and of the knowledge of the Son of God, to a perfect man, to the measure of the stature of the fullness of Christ.
> —EPHESIANS 4:11–13, NKJV

As I've mentioned, the office of prophet is much heavier than the gift of prophecy. The words and the teachings go much deeper.

Micaiah faced off against four hundred so-called prophets who were no more prophets than I am a bus. They held no such office, but they were publicly spun to be such by Ahab and Jezebel. They were bought and paid for; therefore, they could not accurately hear the Lord, nor would the Lord speak to them, because their allegiance was to those who served Baal. Their allegiance was not to the Lord; it was to Jezebel, Ahab, and the horrifically pagan and wicked kingdom they established.

Today, the internet is saturated with those who say they hold the office of a prophet, who have been propped up by others marketing them as such. Being marketed as a prophet does not mean you hold the office of prophet. Compromised pastors are pushing and peddling prophets who are no such thing. They have opened the wrong gift. Many have tried to steal someone else's gift or someone else's office, but they were never meant to have it. The superficial and vague have taken over a significant part of the prophetic. Again, as prophet Kim Clement would say, the words may be right, but the breath is wrong.

We are facing an oracle-at-Delphi situation in the prophetic where people come seeking a word, and all they get is smoke and mirrors, convulsing, crying, and superficial, vague words. With the vague words the deception of accuracy continues when indeed there is little accuracy or truth to be found. Words of the week and words of the day are purposely spoken in a superficial and vague way so the appearance of being accurate is given. It's all superficial; it's all on the surface. The roots do not run deep. In fact, the roots cannot go deep because the people offering these vague words have attempted to hijack an office they were never meant to be in.

There are individuals heading up ministries who lack discernment and are spiritually compromised in their own lives, and they see these propped-up "prophets" as a way to get people to watch them and support them, as a way to grow their platforms. These people may have been propped up, but in this time, the Lord is going to kick that prop out from under them. There is a huge difference between the prophetic and a flashy salesman with snake oil promising you everything in a bottle. There is a huge difference between a shepherd and a showman.

The prophetic has been tainted not only with false prophecy and vague prophecy but also with junk intel. Someone who truly holds the office of a prophet is very careful about how much they watch fake news, corrupt news, corrupt teachers, and other sources of intel. For those of us who hold the office of prophet, God is supposed to be the source, not anonymous sites, junk intel, or those who claim to have legitimate sources that are actually corrupt! When people fill their souls with such things, it does not take long for these "prophecies" to sound just as those corrupt sources do. In fact, some who call themselves prophets are deep diving into junk intel, writing their so-called prophecies from it, and then publicly claiming that they came from the Lord! It's the same gig that Ahab's prophets had, except in a modern time.

Many so-called prophets have become just like that feeble old man hiding behind a curtain and claiming to be the "great and powerful" Oz. There are also those going back to the past words of other prophets, taking some of the content for themselves, and manipulating the words to present them as words they received themselves. One cannot accurately prophesy from a place of deception. Prophecy is grounded in truth. Prophecy's foundation is truth because the words of the Lord are truth. Any prophecy with a foundation of deception is false prophecy.

Prophecy is meant to edify, exalt, and warn. A believer with the office of prophet is also meant to teach. The results should be people pressing in deeper with the Lord and glory being brought to His name. Prophecy should point people to the Lord, not to the prophet. Prophecy should bring glory to the Lord, not the prophet.

The Old Testament is filled with examples of prophets and prophecies causing people to press in deeper with the Lord and to bring glory to His name. Remember the result of Elijah's showdown with the false prophets on Mount Carmel? It wasn't "Wow, Elijah the prophet is amazing. I wonder if he has a word for me." Rather, the children of Israel fell on their faces and cried out, "The LORD, He is God! The LORD, He is God!" (1 Kings 18:39).

Prophecy should always go back to the Word. The Lord is the Word, so He will quote Himself! Also, prophecy should not sound like the person delivering it. What do I mean by this? The Lord has His own way of communicating. Almighty God is a separate power and entity from man, but He works through man. Therefore, the way the Lord views events happening in the earth and events to come is from a heavenly view, not an earthly view. The Lord's perspective is outside space and time as we know it.

I am an Italian from the Bronx in New York. But when I give a word from the Lord, it should not sound like a Bronx Italian. God is not a Bronx Italian, and I am not God; therefore, the prophetic word should be spoken the way the Lord wants it said, not the way I speak every day to my family and friends. It should be the Lord's words and the Lord's choice of delivery. It is about what the Lord wants to say, not about what we want to hear. We are merely the messengers and the vessels through whom such a word is spoken.

The prophetic is in need of a deep clean, and I believe in the coming years we will see that happen. The Lord is calling believers holding that office, as well as others who are part of the fivefold ministry, deeper. A maturing is necessary. Those who want to stay in the superficial, vague, and tainted will find themselves wading in a shallow, dirty puddle, and that is where they will stay if they continue their games, their shows, at the expense of God's Word. This is a clarion call in this time for the fivefold ministry to be cleansed, for the prophetic office to experience a deep clean, and for our roots to go deeper and wider for the purposes of God and advancing His kingdom on this earth.

CHAPTER 5

THE WARRIORS OF THE NEW MILLENNIUM

BY DONNÉ CLEMENT PETRUSKA

THE YEAR WAS 1993, and we had just moved to Texas from South Africa. The adjustment had been difficult. We did not want to leave our home and family, but we also knew God had given my dad, Kim Clement, a special gift and that it helped a lot of people, so we understood why we needed to go.

We moved to a house in the suburbs outside Dallas. The Dallas Fort Worth International Airport and the Dallas area are in a central location in the United States, and because Dad had to travel so much, with his ministry being completely itinerant at that stage, it was a perfect location for our family to settle.

Dad tried so hard to make the move easy for us kids. He was like a big kid himself sometimes, and he knew we felt strange living in a completely different country and culture. He was always coming up with fun things for us to do as a family. Bike rides were common, but he had taken things up a notch and purchased two motorized bicycles, or mopeds. Each moped was basically a bike with a motor that went up to twenty-five miles per hour on the back and a big red button near the handlebars to cut the engine if needed.

One afternoon he challenged me to a race. We had been doing this frequently since he bought the mopeds, and it was always fun and a laugh. I accepted the challenge, and we hopped on our mopeds and raced off through the neighborhood. We went all through the neighborhood, into the next one, and back again into ours. I had beaten him on the way out, so he challenged me to one last race back to the house. Off we went, laughing and swerving around each other. As we neared the cul-de-sac, he was winning, and he shot ahead of me down the driveway.

There was a huge RV parked in our driveway. It belonged to a friend of my dad's, a bishop named Michael Babin. He had parked his RV at our house for a few weeks, and Dad was racing right toward it. I realized that something was wrong when I noticed he wasn't slowing down. As the moped sped directly for the RV, my dad stuck his leg out and went flying through the air.

I was already off my moped and running toward him by the time he hit the ground. He was unconscious in the driveway, and I thought he was dead. I started screaming for my mother. "Call 911! Call 911!" I yelled as I saw her emerge from the house through the garage.

Dad started to wake up. He sat up, groaning in agony, holding his arm, and looking white as a sheet. My mother immediately put him in the car and drove away with him to the hospital. I stood watching them, and I felt the enemy all around me. I began to pray right there in the driveway where he fell, and the intensity of the atmosphere was heavy and dark. As I prayed against it, I pointed my finger at the place where he fell and bound the enemy in the name of Christ. I felt the heaviness lift, and I could breathe again, but I also knew an attack had been carried out and this was not the end. This was the beginning. It was war.

If anyone knows anything about my dad, they know how well he played the piano. This was a gift he possessed from childhood, and he was a prodigy child. He was playing full pieces by some of the greatest composers by ear when he was five years old. His mother, my grandmother Babette, had named him Kimball after the piano company. This was very prophetic in itself, considering he would become such an amazing pianist.

Both of Dad's wrists were broken in the fall from the moped. He told me afterward that the brakes did not work as he sped toward the driveway, so he tried to hit the big red button to cut the engine, but it did not work. As he realized he was about to drive straight into Michael Babin's RV at top speed, he stuck his leg out and jumped off right in time. He toppled over, landed on his bent wrists, and hit his head on the hard driveway. The impact completely broke all the bones in his right wrist and most of them in his left. They had to do emergency surgery on both of his wrists and hands, and he ended up with screws and bolts connecting his hands to his arms!

While recovering from the surgery that night, Dad had a reaction to a medication they gave him, and he actually started to die. My mother did not tell us kids how bad it really got in the hospital that night; we only found out afterward, but it was terrifying.

It was much later when I heard from Dad what had happened that night and the things God revealed to him while he was under such a brutal attack. The first thing to note is how many things had to happen for that attack to come about. The moped was new, and it had brakes and a giant red button to cut power to the motor. Both of those things failed at the same time. This never happened again with that moped or the other one. It was an isolated incident.

The next thing to note is *where* my dad was injured. He was not just a genius piano player. My dad worshipped on the keys, and his prophetic expression came from that place of worship to God. When he played the piano in worship to God, there was a window opened for him to see beyond the confines of time and space. The enemy attempted—very boldly and aggressively, almost desperately—to close that window.

Because my dad understood this was a spiritual attack, he knew what he had to do. He had to overcome the prognoses that the doctors had spoken over him after his surgery. "You will never play the piano the same again. You will never be able to move your hand from right to left and back again." Either prognosis would have greatly deterred his ability to play the piano and, as a result, his ability to worship God "from the keys," as he was so known to articulate it.

In the hospital that night, after brutally breaking his wrists and then almost dying from an allergic reaction to medication, he had an encounter—with the devil.

Dad said that while he was in the hospital bed, a very nice-looking man in a suit appeared in his room. He knew immediately who this was, and he filled with rage as the man climbed onto the bed and crawled up so he was eventually straddling my dad with his hands pressed on Dad's chest and his nose against my dad's nose.

"So *you* will be piercing the darkness?" It was all my dad heard before he blacked out. In the process of this, the window was blown violently open, and Dad heard a sound. It was a rumbling, a sound like nothing he had ever heard before. It was the sound of a mighty army. He saw a horizon, and he could hear the sound approaching. Suddenly, he began to see young people whom God was using. They were an unexpected group of people; they did not look like typical Christians. They were tattooed and pierced, they spoke roughly and bluntly, and they were covered in battle scars and wounds. From their lips came the sound of a name: "Yeshua! Yeshua!" It was deafening, and this was an army unlike anything Dad had ever seen. Then he heard their name. These were the Warriors of the New Millennium!

In his autobiography, *Call Me Crazy, but I'm Hearing God*, Dad describes these events.

> Over the next few days, I began seeing things beyond the year 2000. For five hours in the night, I had visions of so many things; and then, finally, I saw a company of young people, and when they shouted, they sounded like people going to war. I saw them wounded, even though they were young, but they were radical, revolutionary, and non-religious. Suddenly, I heard God speak to me, and He said, "You are seeing a generation of prophets who will emerge from the dust and become an army..."
>
> This was a turning point in my life, and it changed my whole expression. When God spoke to me through the visions in the night, I saw the ones I call the Warriors of the New Millennium. I saw those who would shake the nations far into the new millennium.[1]

This was a turning point in my dad's life, and we saw him emerge from that experience with a stronger prophetic gift and an understanding of the gravity of what God had shown him. He began to recover at home from his injuries. He had both of his arms in casts, which made life extremely difficult, especially for him. He was a busy man, independent, restless, and driven; having to rely on others to help him was almost unbearable, but he suffered through it.

When the casts came off, he immediately returned to his piano and began defiantly to play it. As the doctors had warned, he struggled to move his hands the way he used to, but he did it anyway. He prayed as he played, and even though it hurt him, he forced his hands to move the way they had before.

Months passed, and he got better and stronger. By the time he was ready to get back on the road and back to ministry at the very long list of churches that had sent him invitations, he was a new man. He had let his hair grow out, and he stopped wearing suits altogether. He began to take on the form and the attitude of the warriors he had seen in the future. But best of all, he played the piano better than he had before—because God had healed him.

It was to the Detroit area that God sent him. He was actually in Dearborn, Michigan, which has one of the largest Muslim populations in America today. It was from Dearborn in 1996, three years after the accident, that he would prophesy 9/11 in a hotel. The prophecy was at an event he held that he named the Gathering of the Dangerous, or GOD. I was there with him at that event, and I was there when he prophesied about the planes that would fly over Long Island in New York, about the "king of the East," and about how this would be the "mother of wars."[2]

To understand the political, social, spiritual, cultural, and economic revolution that we are experiencing in this time, we have an advantage in the realm of prophecy. For those of us who have been there to witness a prophet at the time he was prophesying, we look back from the moment we are currently in, and suddenly there are answers to questions. Suddenly, we see more clearly, we discern more sharply, and the image from the future begins to emerge for us. This is like military intelligence for spiritual warfare.

The way God works is not just incredible—it is unmatchable. I am in awe every day as I see through social media or see on the news or hear in conversations the echo of my father's voice prophesying the moment I am standing in now. God sent my dad, among a select few, to prepare America for a war as we have never seen. But this message is one of hope and of victory in a sea of descending voices that constantly berate and cast doubt on the masses.

Something my dad taught me has to do with perception. The way we perceive the moment we are in can determine the outcome. If we are endlessly fed images, sounds, and feelings that are against God's will, it is impossible for us to see or even accept God's will. God sends *His* prophets to speak the future into our present circumstances. So when we saw Donald Trump arrested and threatened with jail, although God said, through my dad, that we would have him "at [the] helm for two terms," it seemed impossible, especially after the 2020 election and how that turned out![3] Yet the prophecy was still fulfilled. This is where the spiritual warfare comes in, where the strategy involved when dealing with prophecy on the battlefield comes in.

When things seem to be at their worst, proclaim what was prophesied into the atmosphere! The way I have done this with my dad's prophecies has been to combat the reports of the enemy with the promise in what was prophesied. When they threaten us with pandemics and incurable diseases, I post prophecies about the cures that will be discovered for Alzheimer's disease, cancer, autism, and diabetes.

To combat the level of warfare we have endured so far requires another level of prophetic training and ability. The prophetic army my dad saw in the visions more than thirty years ago is currently occupying territory for Christ, but the time for true unity has come.

On February 22, 2014, my dad prophesied about the same army he had seen in 1993:

> This man that I saw in the vision, a man that came out of a vision, please hear me. I was standing in my garden. Suddenly the Spirit came and removed from my eyes, scales. I was praying for America, and I was praying for Israel, nothing unusual. Suddenly behind me, starting behind my back, going in the form of an arrow, were hundreds of thousands of people. And I turned around and I was stunned at what I saw. This was not just a mere dream, but this was a vision. And so I raised my hand like this, and every one of them raised their hands. I looked back, and they were doing the same thing. I shouted, and they all shouted. They were one; they were one; one party, one party of people. It continued until I realized that [in] the unity of these, amongst them stood one that God had set aside to be the leader of this nation.[4]

In 2014 this prophecy did not make sense. In 2024 we can immediately identify Trump and the "Make America great again" (MAGA) movement. With scales removed from our eyes, we can identify it as the awakening, or being red pilled. The key takeaway from this prophecy is that it combats the woke culture and the division that politicians in both parties constantly use to retain their power and control. This prophecy also shows that the answer to the tactic of division is unity. But we can't just be united. We have to be united *under God*. We can't be united under lies, so we must be united in our search for *truth*, even the hard truth that is difficult to face.

Jesus told us very clearly that He is the way, the truth, and the life. If we cannot get to the Father unless through Him, then the banner we carry must be the banner of Jesus Christ.

TRAINING THE ARMY

So how does an army of millennial warriors train? First, we must put on the whole armor of God. (See Ephesians 6.) Our sin is our weakness, and our weakness is a way for the enemy to strike us. Now more than ever we must resist the weaknesses of the flesh. And when we recognize weaknesses in one another, it must not be a way to judge one another and fall into self-righteousness, but rather it is an opportunity to help our fellow soldiers, as we would on the battlefield.

But there is more that is needed of us.

These are unprecedented times, and that calls for unprecedented spiritual training. A crucial part of this training, the most important in this hour, is the gift of prophecy. When looking at this ascension gift as simply a way to see the future, we miss how much more we can use it in battle. If the warriors are all in tune with God's rhythm, are all praying—speaking to Him and listening to Him—and are all acute at recognizing God's voice and quickly obeying it, then God, and only God, will be leading the army.

My dad saw a revolution. He saw God's people working in a new way, moving through the streets and abandoning meaningless ritual for true Christianity that stands on the foundation of the first-century faith. That level of faith has come to be needed again as we head into a battle mankind has never seen.

And as the battle rages in the heavenlies, so the nations of the earth rage now. It is the people of earth against the devil himself. His handiwork no longer is ambiguous but has become unavoidable as he has convinced mankind they are evil and they are nothing more than food for AI. The devil freely murders life in the womb, and he corrupts, openly and brutally, the bodies of children. He has caused confusion and corrupted everything with greed and filth. It is the innocent who suffer, and it is for them that we must fight.

I remember that day in 1993. I was so young, but I was a witness, as I have been so many times in my life, to the warfare that rages in the spirit. I saw and experienced direct and vicious attacks of an enemy who has become so bold because we have allowed it—thus the necessity to wake up, face the truth, and kick the devil's butt!

God will never leave us or forsake us, and He has a plan for these times. He told us through my dad and others what we need to know. Now it is up to us. Will we humble ourselves and let go of the need to be right? Will we love and forgive our enemies? Will we be transformed by the renewing of our minds? I think we can, but I know we will because God showed us the victory before the war.

CHAPTER 6

THE SPIRIT OF PYTHOS

BY DONNÉ CLEMENT PETRUSKA

MY DAD HAD a stroke on Labor Day in 2015. The date was September 7. It was a huge shock because Dad was the picture of health. He ate well—no red meat, no bread, no sugar. He was extremely disciplined and in control of himself. There was no warning except some high blood pressure, which was hereditary and was not really a surprise or a serious problem.

Because my dad was a prophet in the *office* of prophet, his prophetic abilities went beyond his standing up and prophesying with words. His music as he worshipped, when the prophecy [often] began, sounded like what he would later prophesy. Perhaps it was joyful or sad, or maybe it carried the beat of a war drum and the rage of men. It was as though the ground were plowed with praise so the seed of the future could be planted and emerge from his mouth after passing through his hands—on a piano, which has strings as a harp, which is reminiscent of King David.

Prophecy is always woven together into a tapestry that projects an image or images, and when more than one true prophet of the Lord sees the same thing, it is of utmost importance that we pay careful attention to this. It is more than confirmation, especially in times such as these.

My dad was attacked viciously. The night before Labor Day of 2015, he was praying in his garden. His prayer garden was a section of his backyard. He had planted a row of trees to section it off as an area to pray. There were so many huge trees, and there was a mountain in the background. There was a brick wall around his property, and his garden was in the corner, tucked away.

He emerged from the garden as the last of the sun disappeared on the horizon, and everything was red and blue as night descended. He walked across the yard to the back patio, where my grandmother Gloria, my mother's mother, sat at the table while my mother ran in and out with dishes and plates of food.

Dad looked alarmed, and my grandmother asked him what was wrong. My dad answered her with a question: "Is it bad if you see a snake when you are praying?"

It seems like a simple, almost obvious question when I think of it now. My grandmother told him yes, it would be a bad thing. She recalled her mother telling her that seeing a snake was a bad omen. My dad then told my grandmother that as he was finishing his prayer and about to leave the garden, he suddenly saw the image of two giant black snakes coming directly at him. It startled him so much that he fell over onto the ground. He felt fearful in his most favorite and sacred place, and he left it, never to return.

The next day he had a stroke. I have struggled to relay what occurred that day without an extreme amount of anxiety and panic. Because of this I am not ready to speak of the details of that day, especially the thing I had to face in that garden the very next night. It was this that changed my perspective forever. My understanding of spiritual warfare was then as a participant. I was no longer only a witness to the reality of the spiritual battle. For the first time in my life I understood what I had only pondered before. In one day everything about our lives changed forever, and we carry the scars of that battle wherever we go.

Years later I heard another prophet speak of seeing in a vision two serpents swimming toward him in water. This immediately got my attention, and the hairs stood up on my arms and the back of my neck. Not long after, another prophetic voice sounded the alarm: two snakes. I remembered Pythos.

The image of the serpent appeared again in the human story. This time two serpents were wrapped around a staff as a pandemic gripped the world. It was the tyranny that never died after the world wars; it was the Fourth Reich rising. It was the same as in the days of Noah when God's creation, the human genome, our unique DNA, was corrupted. It was happening once again.

Sometimes when my dad prophesied, applicable verses spoken by the prophets of old would come out. Some that he commonly quoted in accordance with the rise of the Fourth Reich—events surrounding the European Organization for Nuclear Research (CERN), the United Nations (UN), the World Health Organization (WHO), and the Geneva region of Switzerland, where the CERN and WHO are headquartered—are from the prophet Isaiah and are specifically about the fall of Lucifer.

> How you are fallen from heaven, O Lucifer, son of the morning! How you are cut down to the ground, you who weakened the nations! For you have said in your heart: "I will ascend into heaven, I will exalt my throne above the stars of God; I will also sit on the mount of the congregation on the farthest sides of the north; I

will ascend above the heights of the clouds, I will be like the Most High."

—ISAIAH 14:12–14, NKJV

Sometimes the words of Jesus Himself came through my dad's songs and prophecies as he completely submitted to God, having more faith than I have ever seen in a person and having the boldness to take a step when no one else would have. He wrote a prophecy in song, quoting Jesus from Luke 10:18 (NKJV): "I saw Satan fall like lightning from heaven." The best part, though, is in verse 19, where Jesus says, "Behold, I give you the authority to trample on serpents and scorpions, and over all the power of the enemy, and nothing shall by any means hurt you" (NKJV).

My dad taught extensively on the spirit of Pythos, and his study and teaching series came as a result of things he began to understand after multiple visions of a python. Dad did a study on the characteristics of a python. The python is very large and has poor eyesight. While it uses its tongue to detect prey, it also uses pits located on its jaws. The pits have heat sensors that allow the python, which is an ambush predator, to know when to strike because it senses the heat coming from the flesh of its prey. Just as the python is attracted to the flesh of its prey, so the spirit of Pythos is attracted to flesh, or sin. If we are to enter into battle, we *must* have an understanding of some foundational concepts. The serpent is attracted to sin.

Another characteristic of the python is the manner in which it kills its prey. The python is a constrictor, so it suffocates its victims. Think of the parallels to what happened during COVID-19, such as people on ventilators and wearing masks. So the spiritual and physical wars align again.

We face an enemy that is governed not by God's law but by the laws of men, of flesh. So the ancient spirit slithered toward the prey it detected, and it began to devour. But God showed my dad something in a vision: an eagle.

Following, I include my dad's account of the vision of Pythos he had on a very specific date, November 5, 2012.

> Let us pray for the soul of America that has been pierced deeply—not only by sinners, not only by those who are God-haters or atheists—but religious people have also pierced the soul of this nation, and I want that to be restored.
>
> Early this morning, I was very restless as I told you in my email. I really struggled to sleep. I began praying, and this doesn't happen a lot. I was caught up into the Spirit and I was surrounded by so much darkness. It was a terrible place to be. Fear gripped me and just for a few seconds, I could see nothing. I was completely blind. Everything was dark; everything was foreboding and dismal. I waited to hear something, and this is the hard thing, that I saw nothing, I heard nothing. It was deathly still. I can't explain to you—not the sound of a whisper, not the sound of wind, not the sound of a bird. Nothing. It was so barren. Have you ever been in a dream where you want to get out of the dream? This was not just a regular dream. This was a dream that was given to me, a vision, by God. Taken to a place where the enemy has planned for our children and this nation. "Kim, you're preaching gloom." Hold on.
>
> I forced myself; I said, "I've got to get out of this place. I've got to get out of here," and I did. When I came around, I was shaking, I was perspiring; I was completely wet, soaked. I forced myself to get back to sleep. I had to get rest; when this happens, it drains the life out of you. I realized that I'd been standing in a land surrounded by absolute darkness—infertile, barren. I

cried out to the Lord and I said, "What is this place?" I heard nothing....I received absolutely no answer.

I got back to sleep for maybe two hours, and I went to my garden where I pray every day, sometimes for hours, and immediately when I entered what I call the "sacred garden" for my morning watch, I received a vision and I stood in one place. I must make this known to you, that I've been healed of a serious back injury, but there are times, when I stand for a long time, that my body starts to ache. But I stood in that one place for so long, literally shaking, and I'm not a "shaker"...but I shook as the Spirit of God came upon me and I realized that there is a great spiritual battle taking place right now, in the heavens. Is this about another leader? No! This is about what is happening in the heavens. It must be spiritually deterred, and spiritually dealt with, and the church is sitting back, for the most part, predicting the end of the world, giving no answers—not praying with fervency and shaking the heavens like Daniel did. And I realized that the burden was upon me, and of course many others that are upright people called to do this, but I realized that because I prophesied so much about this nation that it was in my hands to pray.

I didn't know what to pray. I just stood there shaking. Then suddenly, it happened—I was taken, and the vision came. I saw a large snake. I knew that the snake was a non-venomous snake but it was extremely dangerous...this snake was extremely dangerous. My understanding was that it was a python. After that, I heard these words: "royal serpent." Now royal sounds great, but serpent doesn't. I looked at the snake, and it was so real, just like this piece of paper in front of me. The snake was a python, and the color was like a reddish color. I don't know much about pythons—all I know is that I don't like them.

During the few moments of terror that I experienced, I was drawn into a maze of words and thoughts, and I heard whispers. My first reaction when I saw this was to run from this dragon. But as I looked around in my garden, if you've been there or seen me in the garden, there are various exits—exit to the road, exit into the house area. The exits were all closed. I couldn't go anywhere. It was almost like I was standing in the state of America. Every exit was shut. I had no choice but to confront this large, non-venomous snake that could do great damage. That's what I want to speak to you about. The vision goes into great detail, which I'll give you now.

I also had perfect understanding that this creature was about 12 feet in length. What was amazing to me was the vapors that were emerging from it. Please try to imagine with me, you are standing, you're literally seeing it. In other words, sometimes when you have a dream, you know it's real. You wake up afraid; you carry that dream sometimes for days. This was a true vision. There were vapors emerging from this python and it seemed like this creature had the power to prophesy. The more that I listened, the more I struggled to breathe. The creature was looking at me, and there were vapors coming from it, and there were different aromas and bad smells. But I listened, and it seemed that permeating from it were prophecies, predictions—and the more I listened, the more I struggled to breathe. I was being suffocated by words, by lies, by deceit, by divination.

This spirit was speaking great swelling words of deceit. I realized this was not just the secular world, or the secular political world, but the religious world as well. They had combined forces, and this thing had tricked them on each side to say the things they're saying today, offering absolutely no hope for America.

Suddenly, I was surrounded by the various states in the United States of America, and this vapor was causing my surroundings to rot. Everything was beginning to rot, to get rotten, from the vapors. What was happening was, it was going through the states; things were rotting everywhere.

Let me explain to you what a python is. Pythons are constrictors. They grab their prey with their teeth then they wrap coils of their bodies around their prey and they squeeze. That's what they do. They take their time and they squeeze. They don't actually crush their prey. I know that as a fact because I taught this in the School of the Prophet, about the actual python. It doesn't actually crush the prey and break its bones; instead, it squeezes tightly so that the prey can't breathe, and it suffocates.

They want the whole delicious body; that's what they want. They want to spit out bones. They squeeze until it suffocates. The spirit that is upon this nation, and the vapors that are permeating from all sectors, are causing a suffocation upon the nation, upon the people, upon our education, upon our economy, upon our morals. I know it's nothing new but how much more can we take of this? What is our responsibility? I'm still in the vision....

I was paralyzed at that stage. I was standing in my garden, but no garden to be seen. I was standing somewhere in the middle of the United States with the states surrounding me, close to Pennsylvania. I was standing in this place, petrified, paralyzed; I could not move, and I was begging, in my spirit, in my heart, saying, "Please, I want out of this, God. What's going on?" Strangely, I constantly heard the sound of a frog croaking, over and over. It sounded like it was a dangerous, large frog. Unfortunately, I have no further understanding of this. But there's something about this noise that I heard. Suddenly, I was approached by this python. I was paralyzed—you know what that's like when you're trying to get away and thinking, "Is this real?" I realized as it approached me that it was protecting eggs that it had laid.

At that point, I felt God's presence all over me, and then I heard the sound of a bird in the sky, a large bird. The python was right in front of me; I noticed the eggs; I notice[d] the python was trying to protect the eggs. I heard the sound of a large bird. Then the python returned to the eggs.

The python returned to the eggs and a strange thing happened. It seemed like the python was coughing or choking, or had hiccups. I was terrified but felt some strength as I heard some words proceeding from a mist or thin cloud that was close to me at that point in time. Then suddenly the vision ended, to my relief, and I fell in my garden. I was standing on the actual stones, which we put there—I actually fell on those stones and lay there. I must have laid there for 45 minutes, completely drained. The vision ended, but my ability to grasp the words that I had heard from heaven [was] strong. It had been deposited.

There's one thing you need to understand. When the Holy Spirit comes upon you and you get something, something is deposited in you that you don't understand at all, but the whole day—when I say the entire day, I mean the entire day—I prayed.

I prayed for the rest of the day, and this is what came to me: a spiritual darkness, specific darkness, came upon this nation, America, and many nations as a result of disobedience to the conditions that God had laid out. This spirit, which is the spirit of divination, has bred scorn and deceit and has not only suffocated the nation in so many areas, but laid fresh eggs in great anticipation that it will not be stopped because of the emasculation of the people of God in prayer and spiritual warfare. The word of the Lord came to me. "Unless the python is removed from the eggs, the suffocation will grow so severe, that the hopes, prayers and dreams of America's enemies will be fulfilled; the destruction of this nation."

I was then reminded of the bird that was in the sky in my vision; it was an eagle. The words that I heard then—"Is it by your understanding that the hawk soars and spreads his wings towards the south?" I'm going to say that again. This is what I heard: "Is it by your understanding that the hawk soars and spreads his wings towards the south? Is it at your command that the eagle mounts up and makes his nest on high? On the rock he dwells and makes his home and on the broken rock has his stronghold, and from there he spies out the prey; his eyes behold it from far away."

I thought about it over and over and it was so clear. If there is no rock, that great soaring eagle cannot come to rest its feet to look for the prey. Christ is the rock and unless that broken, strong rock is exalted on high, there will be no victory. Unless Israel is loved, honored and protected, there will be no victory and suffocation will take its toll in a very different, severe manner. That's the vision that I had.

Leviticus 19:26 and 31 [paraphrased]: "You shall not practice divination" and "give no regard to familiar spirits and do not seek after them to be defiled by them." Suffocation has come to us. We are affected;

every home is affected except for those that may have taken authority, but America is on the pathway to light. The eggs will be crushed when people stand together and cry out for the Rock of Ages to be exalted [and when] people pray and they take the word of the Lord seriously and say, "We will do what God asked us to do." 300 men with Gideon destroyed tens of thousands of the armies. Jehoshaphat, with a few priests raising their hands after a prophet had spoken, completely overcame the enemy.[1]

Within the vision are a warning, a strategy, and a hopeful end, but there are requirements of *us*. God is not telling us to sit back with popcorn and watch Him work. He is calling us to join Him in battle because the victory is contingent on our humility, faith, obedience, and capacity to exist in a state that is not dictated by this dusty world we find ourselves in.

God gives us the prophetic as a tool, a weapon, an answer when no answer can be found. When in the thick of spiritual warfare, of a war that is truly revelationary, only an army of prophets will suffice.

We are the warriors of the new Millennium, and although our enemy has quietly planned for many years, God had a plan so brilliant it could have come only from *Him*, through us, at the perfect time.

That time is upon us.

CHAPTER 7

THE COLOSSEUM OF TECHNOLOGY AND MEDIA

T**HE COLOSSEUM IS** a large amphitheater that was built in the center of ancient Rome. It held up to eighty thousand spectators who watched gladiators fight and other public spectacles, such as executions, plays, and battle reenactments. The design of the Colosseum was meant to draw one's eyes and attention to the viciousness happening at the center. The Colosseum was built to draw the eyes of people down to what was happening on the arena floor, which was the stage for whatever show was happening.

The Colosseum still stands today in the center of Rome, although it has been significantly damaged over the years. Yet there is another colosseum in our world today. It is an amphitheater that draws our eyes and attention to the show, to the whole lot of lie mixed with a little bit of truth that the kingdom of darkness uses to deceive us and draw us away from the Lord.

Billy Graham wrote in 1954, "Has it ever occurred to you that the Devil is a religious leader and millions are worshipping at his shrine today?"[1] This statement made in the 1950s has never been more true than it is today. The shrines the devil has erected are massive, influential, and drawing people in, alluring them into the enslavement of his religion.

Media and technology are two of these shrines. They are the colosseum of the enemy.

MEDIA

The English word *media* can be traced back through Latin to a Greek word referring to a region in the Middle East as well as to a figure in Greek mythology.

The region called Media is located in northwestern Iran and is most known as the cultural and political base of the ancient Medes.[2] Why is this so important to note? In the Book of Daniel, King Darius—who overthrew Belshazzar, a descendant of King Nebuchadnezzar—was a Mede. The overthrow occurred after a hand literally appeared at a feast Belshazzar was hosting and wrote on the wall, "MENE, MENE, TEKEL, UPHARSIN," meaning "God has numbered your kingdom, and finished it....You have been weighed in the balances, and found wanting....Your kingdom has been divided, and given to the Medes and Persians" (Dan. 5:25–28, NKJV). King Belshazzar was killed that very night. After all this occurred, the Mede magicians and officials who were put in charge of the kingdom schemed and planned to destroy Daniel through a campaign of persecution and disinformation. (See Daniel 5:29–6:23.)

In Greek mythology there was an enchantress, or sorceress, named Medea. Although not a goddess herself, she was believed to be of divine descent because her father was the son of the sun god Helios. She was also a priestess of Hecate, a goddess associated with magic, witchcraft, and the night. Medea is connected to this digital colosseum in which we find ourselves in the current day. She personified ideologies and beliefs that lead the masses away from relationship with the Lord and into the controlling cycle of the world system.

Medea was a spirit who was a planner, a schemer, and a sorceress. She was willing to betray to achieve a desired outcome. Sorcery has to do with spells. It is interesting how this subtly finds its way into everyday life. Proverbs 18:21 says, "Death and life are in the power of the tongue, and those who love it will eat its fruit" (NKJV). Medea used her mouth to speak curses. The tongue can curse, or it can bless. The enemy understands this concept well and has built his kingdom of darkness with the curses that proceed from the mouths of humanity. Is it any wonder that in the arena of media today, the arena's heads are schemers, planners, and sorcerers utilizing sensationalism, deception, and smoke and mirrors to entice humanity to buy into their lies? Is it any wonder that the enemy uses those same tactics in the media to get people to subscribe to the false doctrines being perpetuated?

This is part of a very dark army that has prophets of Baal, sorcerers, and crafty magicians, just as in Daniel's day. They perpetuate lies; they repeat them over and over. They operate the same way the serpent did at the tree in the Garden of Eden. Their lies are meant to cause doubt that will nullify the truth. They use their evil ideologies, their digital propaganda, and their falsehoods to mesmerize the people, to try to make them believe that a skewed idea is true. Remember, the enemy always mixes the whole lot of lie with a little bit of truth to make the lie appear credible. The little bit of truth comes first in order to hook people, and then the enemy brings in a lie to close the deal and bring people into bondage.

Medea was also a mocker. She used her words to cut down and undermine others. The leaders of ancient Rome used the same strategy with the ancient Jews. The land we now know as Palestine was named Judea before ancient Rome, named after the kingdom and tribe of Judah, from which the Messiah was promised to (and did!) come. The Romans changed the name of the region from Judea to Palestine (named after the Philistines, the enemies of the children of Israel) to mock the Jewish people, to punish them, and to attempt to break the covenant tie between the Jews and the Promised Land, the land of Israel. It was part of the Romans' campaign to water down and replace what the Lord had named the nation and what He had called it to be.

This is similar to what we see happening in the modern-day generation. The enemy is using the media and other tools to try to undermine what God and His Word have spoken. It is a continual psychological campaign of propaganda against the minds of those in this nation and throughout the earth. This campaign is well planned and well funded, and it bows to the beast from a dark abyss. Media, at the core, look for ways to curse God and destroy or redefine morality. Media's mockery of the ways of the Lord, of the truth of the Word of God, and of the believers who are faithfully serving the Lord plants doubt and even fear in people's minds. The enemy knows that to get humanity to abandon truth, he must first make them doubt in their minds what is true. Then the enemy has an unlocked door through which he can enter and cause man to entertain and then accept an alternate way, a way that appeals to the lusts of the flesh rather than the fruit of the Spirit.

Ephesians 4:13–14 (NASB) says,

> Until we all attain to the unity of the faith, and of the knowledge of the Son of God, to a mature man, to the measure of the stature which belongs to the fullness of Christ. As a result, we are no longer to be children, tossed here and there by waves and carried about

by every wind of doctrine, by the trickery of men, by craftiness in deceitful scheming.

"Craftiness in deceitful scheming" could have been written about Medea. Scheming equals Medea, which equals media! The warning in Ephesians describes the very essence of the media today. Trickery, craftiness, and scheming wrap up with a bow what the bulk of the media engages in. When Donald Trump called them fake news, he hit the nail on the head! They're a scheme, they are fake, and they allure man to come into agreement with the fabricated. The media can twist and turn a false reality so it appears true. The media have the propensity to get the masses to come into agreement with lies. The media manipulate the minds of viewers so they take a bite, just as Adam and Eve did, and accept what is false as true. The lie is offered through vessels who have committed themselves to the false revelation, and they in turn feed it to multitudes. This is unfolding from the tree of the knowledge of good and evil on a mass scale.

One other thing to note about the sorceress Medea is she killed her own children. We live in a time when the media are constantly trying to make people think that abortion is OK, that it is not a big deal to kill babies in the womb, and that being able to kill your own children before they are born is a human right. The enemy comes to steal, kill, and destroy, and he uses the media to make people think death and destruction caused by abortion are completely fine. The devil is a liar.

TECHNOLOGY

Technology is the media's partner in crime. The English word *technology* comes from the Greek word *techne*. The word refers to art, craft, and technical skill. Techne was a component of Greek philosophy, and there were even altars built to honor the spirit of techne.

There are factions of the kingdom of darkness that are technologically advanced beyond what is in the earthly realm. Through willing vessels, they have an open door to push this technology into the earth, to push their dark agenda. They utilize it to get people to worship technology over almighty God. They have set up technology as an idol, an idol whose altar stretches the span of the globe. Humans have massive information available at their fingertips, and giving them the answers they need, or at least think they need, in every area of their lives sets up technology as a counterfeit omniscient being, a being that knows all. It also sets up technology as a false prophet operated by those who are looking to rid the earth of almighty God and His Word.

Why does the kingdom of darkness want to rid the earth of God and His Word? The answer is in the Word of God.

> For the word of God is living and active and full of power [making it operative, energizing, and effective]. It is sharper than any two-edged sword, penetrating as far as the division of the soul and spirit [the completeness of a person], and of both joints and marrow [the deepest parts of our nature], exposing and judging the very thoughts and intentions of the heart.
>
> —Hebrews 4:12

The Word is living, active, sharp, and discerning, and it is everything we need to transform our lives through Jesus Christ and sharpen our sensitivities to the lies, schemes, and attacks of the enemy. The Word of God exposes Satan's strategies, which causes grave damage to his kingdom and his agenda.

The technology battle is now centered on one main thing: AI. It is the battle of AI. In Joshua's day there was a battle of Ai. Joshua sent spies to the city of Ai before the battle, and the spies reported Ai wasn't a big deal. They didn't think Ai had the ability to dominate the people of Israel, and they told Joshua that only a small army was needed. But they were wrong, and the army "fled before the men of Ai," who caused the children of Israel to fear so that "the hearts of the people melted and became like water" (Josh. 7:4–5, NKJV).

Ai did have the ability to dominate the people of Israel, and this is the same with the AI of our day. What started out as not seeming to have the ability to dominate has done just that. AI is taking dominion in the arena of technology.

After the defeat at Ai, Joshua went before the Lord. He received instructions about how to be victorious in the battle against Ai. The Lord told him,

> Get up, sanctify the people, and say, "Sanctify yourselves for tomorrow, because thus says the LORD God of Israel: 'There is an accursed thing in your midst, O Israel; you cannot stand before your enemies until you take away the accursed thing from among you.'"
>
> —JOSHUA 7:13, NKJV

Joshua had to consecrate himself and the camp to the Lord and purge the camp of sin so they could go back and defeat Ai. We must do the same. It is time for the church to sanctify itself, to consecrate itself before the Lord. It is time to purge the sin in our camp so we can stand before our enemies in victory.

On May 3, 2023, there was an article in The Times of Israel that reported a warning about AI creating religious texts and inspiring cults to form. Yuval Noah Harari, an Israeli historian, philosopher, and known atheist, stated,

> In the future, we might see the first cults and religions in history whose revered texts were written by a non-human intelligence....For thousands of years, prophets and poets and politicians have used language and storytelling in order to manipulate and to control people and to reshape society....Now AI is likely to be able to do it. And once it can...it doesn't need to send killer robots to shoot us. It can get humans to pull the trigger.[3]

Even an atheist recognizes the danger.

There exists an entire ecosystem spiritually and in the natural that supports the beast of media and its perpetual lies. This faction of the kingdom of darkness has pushed onto the earth, honing and shaping this operation for thousands of years. Instead of a talking serpent wrapped around a tree that the Lord said was forbidden, it's now a talking program—or a talking head—still funded and controlled by the same serpent and still enticing people to do what the Lord has said is forbidden. However, the presentation has changed in order to get a modern-day generation to look upon this tempting piece of fruit that is forbidden, in order to lure them to partake in it on a global scale. The same lie of the serpent is being used: "Did God really say...?" These are the false prophets of technology at work for the serpent, and they have especially eyed your children, the younger generation, as a purse prize.

Here it is, the worshipping of AI, a technology created and programmed by corrupt men. It forms new religious texts for humans to bow down to and worship and wipes the mainframes of humanity, which would be our souls and our spirits, of any connection to God. This makes it far easier for the false prophets and rogue shepherds to speak lies that sound similar to a higher conscious truth. The more they can strip humanity's ability to discern the voice of the Lord from the voice of the serpent, the more the enemy can put humanity into bondage—and they will not even know it is happening until it's too late.

THE COLOSSEUM

If we look at the way media, especially social media, are structured, media really are a modern-day digital colosseum where deception is a sport and persecuting the Word of God and the people of God is a public spectacle. The colosseum of media and technology is meant to draw attention to the viciousness happening in the arena. The whole Roman Colosseum was built to draw the eyes of the spectators to the show taking place on the arena floor, to the point that they were not aware of what was happening around them because they were distracted by the fighting and drawing of blood happening in the pit. They lost sight of who was actually steering and directing the show taking place before their eyes—the corrupt officials in high government positions who pledged their allegiance to false gods and wanted to appease their gods. They were actively desensitizing the people of that day to violence. In fact, they groomed them to cheer for it and for their flesh to want it.

What is taking place in the media today is psychological bombardment to sear the conscience and desensitize the souls and spirits of humanity. The goal is to make the immoral and unrighteous seem moral and righteous so humanity no longer desires or follows the foundational beliefs of Christianity, so humanity no longer desires to love, follow, or serve God Most High. This is a colosseum where talking heads, faceless avatars, rogue shepherds, and corrupt prophets all attempt to get your eyes and attention on what satisfies the flesh while deceiving the mind.

This is a colosseum where the main artery between sin and conviction is severed and sin is not called out for the snake it is. Instead, the deception grows into a giant, taunting and cursing the army of the living God, just as Goliath taunted the army of Israel. The enemy's taunting lies are that God is dead, His Word is tainted, His Word is not living and active, He is not living and active, and He is not all-powerful. The enemy steers men into the trap of the tree.

At the tree of the knowledge of good and evil a trap was set, and a revelationary war was declared. Through the generations, the trap of the tree keeps getting reset with another tempting piece of fruit. Ever since the tree, every generation of man has found themselves facing that trap, the trap that says that you don't need to listen to and obey God, that God didn't really mean what He said, that there is an alternate way to live an abundant life, and that other gods can give you what you want. All those lies are part of the enemy's trap, deceiving his prey into believing they can circumvent submitting to the Lord of hosts and His righteous law.

The idea that man can do whatever they want was the foundation of the belief system of the people who built the Tower of Babel. It was an alternative way, a new so-called revelation, that discarded God and the truth that He is the Almighty, He is all-powerful, and He is the Creator of the earth, of all that is seen and unseen. The enemy wants to make you believe God is not as powerful as His Word has said and He is just trying to keep you from becoming like Him, which is why He doesn't want you to indulge in all these tantalizing treats. Since the enemy wars in cycles, this dangerous lie has been recycled through the generations more than a soda bottle ever has been!

In our modern day not only has the lie been recycled again, but it has mutated and branched off into a digital guerrilla warfare where the false prophets now have avatars, YouTube channels, X accounts, podcasts, and blogs. Those faces on the major network news are just the front men and women who hide the ones making the decisions about what hypnotizing ideas of darkness, hopelessness, and propaganda are peddled.

Enter a major weapon in the revelationary war—Operation Mockingbird.

OPERATION MOCKINGBIRD

According to Wikipedia,

> Operation Mockingbird is an alleged large-scale program of the United States Central Intelligence Agency (CIA) that began in the early years of the Cold War and attempted to manipulate domestic American news media organizations for propaganda purposes. According to author Deborah Davis, Operation Mockingbird recruited leading American journalists into a propaganda network and influenced the operations of front groups. CIA support of front groups was exposed when an April 1967 *Ramparts* article reported that the National Student Association received funding from the CIA. In 1975, Church Committee Congressional investigations revealed Agency connections with journalists and civic groups.[4]

Operation Mockingbird was exposed by author Deborah Davis in her unauthorized biography of Katharine Graham, former owner of the *Washington Post*. Even before the book was published, some members of the mainstream media with connections to US intelligence did a hard press, including the threat of lawsuits for libel, to discredit the book. The short version of the story is even despite the threats and the allegations that information in the book is false, "the publisher knew of no specific misstatements...and had no reason to think anyone was going to sue for libel." And no one ever did sue for libel over the content of the book.[5] But the campaign against the book does explain the use of the word *alleged* in the Wikipedia article.

The ideas and tactics behind Operation Mockingbird existed long before the operation was ever given such a name. We can look back at the Bible and see that the spirits behind such propaganda have been at work since the tree of the knowledge of good and evil. For instance, just as I mentioned in previous chapters, the four hundred prophets of Ahab all agreed and said the same thing about Ahab and Jehoshaphat going into battle, because a company of voices would give more credibility to the lie being told.

A similar thing happened in the wilderness when Moses faced Korah and a company of voices.

> Now Korah the son of Izhar, the son of Kohath, the son of Levi, with Dathan and Abiram, the sons of Eliab, and On the son of Peleth, sons of Reuben, took action, and they rose up before Moses, together with some of the sons of Israel, two hundred and fifty leaders of the congregation, chosen in the assembly, men of renown. They assembled together against Moses and Aaron, and said to them, "You have gone far enough, for all the congregation are holy, every one of them, and the LORD is in their midst; so why do you exalt yourselves above the assembly of the LORD?"

> When Moses heard this, he fell on his face; and he spoke to Korah and all his company, saying, "Tomorrow morning the Lord will show who is His, and who is holy, and will bring him near to Himself; even the one whom He will choose, He will bring near to Himself. Do this: take censers for yourselves, Korah and all your company, and put fire in them, and lay incense upon them in the presence of the Lord tomorrow; and the man whom the Lord chooses shall be the one who is holy. You have gone far enough, you sons of Levi!"
>
> —Numbers 16:1–7, nasb

The sons (tribe) of Levi were chosen by God to be priests in the temple of the Lord. They were leaders of Israel. But the enemy started working his deception. The priests were corrupted by the lies of the enemy, and they wanted to seize leadership from Moses and take the nation in a direction the Lord did not authorize. These were rogue priests, and the enemy had stirred up them *all* into believing and saying the same thing in an attempt to hijack the leadership of Israel and replace the righteous priests with priests who were inclined to corruption.

Today the tactics of Operation Mockingbird and similar operations are things we should be very aware of as believers. First Peter 5:8 says, "Be of sober spirit, be on the alert. Your adversary, the devil, prowls around like a roaring lion, seeking someone to devour" (nasb).

First of all, what is a mockingbird? Understanding the traits of this animal will shine a light of truth on why this name was intentionally selected.

Wikipedia says mockingbirds "are best known for the habit of some species mimicking the songs of other birds and the sounds of insects and amphibians, often loudly and in rapid succession" and "for being extremely territorial when raising hatchlings."[6] The key traits are mimicking "loudly and in rapid succession" and being territorial. Hmm.

Interestingly enough, if you do not catch the mockingbird in action, you will be deceived into believing the mocking-bird is a dove, a beetle, a bullfrog, or a bluebird. What you hear is a mimicking, a counterfeit. It would take keen discernment to realize the sound is counterfeit, and it would take a willingness to search until you find the source of the sound. The Bible says in Proverbs 25:2, "It is the glory of God to conceal a matter, but the glory of kings is to search out a matter" (NASB). Seeking out the source, finding out who the source is, will tell you the foundational motive of the source's actions. In this day and age discernment is one of the top abilities believers need in order to grow with the Lord and stay grounded in the truth. If you cannot discern, you cannot tell the difference between what is true and counterfeit, between the truth and the lie. As believers we should be very sensitive to the source of information. If the source is a producer within mainstream media that despises the sanctity of God and the truth of His Word, we need to be on our guard against the deception of the enemy.

While Operation Mockingbird was focused on journalists, we know the CIA also targeted student groups with similar tactics. The National Student Association, an association of members of college student governments, was given money by the CIA with instructions to promote their views, the views of the CIA.

Hmm, college students were being paid to try to affect US foreign policy. I wonder if that has anything to do with what we have seen across college campuses in the United States. In 2024 the ideologies of the Palestinians, Hamas, and radical Islam spread like wildfire across college campuses, causing mass protests and disruptions, as well as distraction from the damage our narcoleptic then president was doing. Even lesbian, gay, bisexual, transgender, and queer (LGBTQ+) activists were supporting and promoting the ideas of radical Palestinians and Hamas despite the fact that homosexuals are often targeted for execution by radical Islamists. It's like a web of alliances all tied to a central governing body.

This sounds quite similar to Ahab and Jezebel's 450 prophets of Baal and 400 prophets of Ashtoreth; the prophets were on the payroll of the central leadership to promote propaganda that steered the people of the nation of Israel away from the Lord and morality and into the treacherous waters of idolatry, deception, and grave sin.

Another crucial part to such an operation is to censor the truth. What does it mean to *censor*? We hear this word a lot in our culture. But what does it really mean? *Censor* means "to suppress or delete as objectionable."[7] *Suppress* means "to put down by authority or force, subdue; to keep from public knowledge."[8] When the truth is censored, when the truth is suppressed, it allows deception and lies to gain a foothold. When the truth of the Word of God is suppressed, this allows a replacement theology or ideology to rise in its place. Those lies, that deception, and that replacement theology is then pushed to the forefront and repeated over and over and over in order to convince the people those things are true. When people hear a lie repeated again and again, it can cause them to doubt and reject the truth and then feast on the lie. That is why, again, it is so important that we know the truth of God's Word; we can't discern the lie if we don't know the truth.

I want to focus on Ashtoreth for a moment here. Ashtoreth is the counterpart to Baal. In January 2023 a golden statue that eerily resembles Ashtoreth, also known as Asherah and Ishtar, was placed atop the New York City courthouse. This golden idol was placed there in honor of Supreme Court justice Ruth Bader Ginsburg, who was a huge supporter of the abortion movement. *The New York Times* carried a headline "Move Over Moses and Zoroaster: Manhattan Has a New Female Lawgiver."[9] This was the ancient spirit's announcement that it was advancing to take the territory in New York that the arch of Baal failed to take back in 2016, and it was an announcement that it was going to utilize a female to attempt to ascend to the highest seat in the land in 2024.

Ishtar was a false goddess of fertility and abortion as well as justice and divine law. This spirit was present in King Ahab's court. It was present at Mount Carmel when Elijah faced the prophets of Baal and Ashtoreth before the people of Israel. It was present when Ahab's four hundred false prophets stood before him with King Jehoshaphat and Micaiah, a true prophet of the Lord. This same spirit has been mocking God, undermining His Word, and challenging His laws since the serpent arrived at the tree of the knowledge of good and evil.

We are kidding ourselves if we think this operation somehow disappeared. Today, not only do we see this in the media, but the mockingbird has infiltrated the church as well. Remember, mockingbirds mimic, and they do it loudly in rapid succession—the more they do it, the more believable it becomes. They are also highly territorial.

Some of the church's talking points have started to not only mimic the propaganda of media but also repeat with a great deal of accuracy the ideologies of groups that are venomously opposed to God, His Word, His order, and His ways. These activist groups are attempting to prophesy, as the prophets of Baal and Ashtoreth did, in order to inherently change the church at its core as well as change the nation, a nation whose governing documents are based on Judeo-Christian beliefs and values.

As believers have continued to falter between two opinions, the church has fractured. Part of the church has broken off into a network of leaders around the country who all mimic similar talking points that have roots leading back to the activist groups making it their mission to destroy the foundations of God's Word, faith, morality, and the biological order that has been in place since the beginning of time. This faction of the church is doing what the prophets in Ahab and Jezebel's day did—they are selling out to eat at the table of those offering to fund them, even though the ones offering the money serve a ruthless, false god.

These hate-filled groups have no interest in anyone continuing and maturing in their walk with the Lord. The focus of these groups is to stunt the growth of the body of Christ, to eradicate critical thinking, and ultimately to provide their so-called "right" thinking for the church through the church's ensnared leaders. If you think about it, Jezebel and Ahab's ruling body of 950 false prophets was the loudest and most vocal with its threats and demands that instilled fear and caused an entire nation to err. The fear was so powerful that those such as Obadiah, Elijah, the one hundred prophets hidden in the caves, and the seven thousand who had not bowed a knee to Baal became a minority, although a very effective minority.

This part of the church is bowing at the altars of funding and giving in to public threats, and it's promoting the toxic talking points of prophets and shepherds who *appear* to be credible—but aren't. Their alternative ideologies and their deceptions are being pushed into the body of Christ. It is time for the church to wake up, to reject false prophets and prophecies, and to turn back to the Lord, to the Word of God, to the truth.

THE PROPHETS OF BAAL

Who are the prophets of Baal in modern times? They are individuals connected to deceptive activist groups and government agendas who feed the people ideologies and theologies that oppose the Word of God.

The serpent at the tree of the knowledge of good and evil opposed the Word of God and the commands of the Lord. The prophets in Ahab's court opposed God's Word, God's law, and God's order. As a company they told a wicked, idolatrous king the Lord was just going to hand him victories!

Today the list of groups, movements, and organizations opposing the Word of God is lengthy, including Black Lives Matter (with a founder funded by China),[10] LGBTQ+ (funded by Black Lives Matter),[11] Planned Parenthood (funded by government money, the United Nations Foundation, and companies such as Shell Oil, among others),[12] liberal lobbying groups, and Republican in name only (RINO) lobbying groups. American colleges and universities, funded by many foreign governments,[13] have snake oil salesmen professors promoting secular humanism. Issues that have wormed their way into the church through the prophets of Baal include COVID-19 "vaccinations," Ukraine and obnoxious amounts of foreign aid for it, abortion (the pro-choice side), and the LGBTQ+ agenda, especially the transgender agenda. Other issues and many forms of perversion all have found their way into the faction of the church that will pay to play and be a voice for Ahab, Jezebel, and the serpent.

Agendas in direct opposition to the Word of God begin with a "do what thou wilt" deception that gets developed and strengthened in the incubators of liberal media; Washington, DC; government think tanks; and colleges across our land. It is then covertly integrated into the church, and by the time it is spoken of at the pulpit, it already has a firm grip on believers, prophets, and shepherds.

THE ROOT

Second Timothy 3:1–5 states,

> But understand this, that in the last days dangerous times [of great stress and trouble] will come [difficult days that will be hard to bear]. For people will be lovers of self [narcissistic, self-focused], lovers of money [impelled by greed], boastful, arrogant, revilers, disobedient to parents, ungrateful, unholy and profane, [and they will be] unloving [devoid of natural human affection, calloused and inhumane], irreconcilable, malicious gossips, devoid of self-control [intemperate, immoral], brutal, haters of good, traitors, reckless, conceited, lovers of [sensual] pleasure rather than lovers of God, holding to a form of [outward] godliness (religion), although they have denied its power [for their conduct nullifies their claim of faith]. Avoid such people and keep far away from them.

This passage covers everything we see unfolding today. All these things we have been discussing are like invasive weeds.

In order for weeds to grow and be strong, they have to choke out the seed-bearing plants. Weeds have deep roots. When an invasive weed with deep roots grows and spreads quickly, the other plants are not able to grow and flourish. But you can't just pull up the part of the weed you see. To get rid of an invasive weed, you must go after the root.

Where did this deception come from? What is the root? What are the sources of these false and dark ideologies? One source is a man named Aleister Crowley, who was an occultist and worshipper of the kingdom of darkness. He was also an avid drug user. This vessel of darkness was given an ideology and strategy from the kingdom of darkness that has saturated the media, schools, colleges, and homes, and it also has begun to heavily saturate a faction of the church: "Do what thou wilt shall be the whole of the Law."[14] Do whatever you want, and that's the law. This is a root within the world of media and social media. This ideology went into overdrive during COVID-19, and the enemy has continued its relentless pursuit ever since.

While on his honeymoon in Egypt in 1904 Crowley heard an unclean spirit, which identified itself as Aiwass, speak to him. For three days Crowley wrote down everything the unclean spirit said in a book he called *Liber AL vel Legis*, or *The Book of the Law*. It is the key sacred text of Thelema, a demonic spirit and also the occult movement founded by Crowley.[15]

Egypt was the place where the Lord broke the superpower of the world centuries before with ten plagues and freed His people from bondage. So those ancient territorial spirits and Satan have had a bone to pick ever since. Crowley was a false prophet, a rogue prophet who sold his soul to the kingdom of darkness and was used as a vessel to plant seeds of deception that would grow as an invasive, suffocating weed.

Again, the spirit called itself Aiwass. If you split the name up, it reads *AI was* (artificial intelligence was). The spirit spoke *Liber AL vel Legis*. If you push the first two words together and translate the rest, it reads *liberal law*! If you put it all together, you have two very invasive entities changing the landscape of humanity: AI was liberal law. The kingdom of darkness strategizes long before its time, plants the seed, and then waits for the right generation to water it! In Egypt, where God's law and power prevailed over the plans of the enemy, Liber AL was heard and birthed: "Do what thou wilt shall be the whole of the Law."

Today these ideas are fostered by a company of false voices. They hunt in packs; they attack in packs. These voices that promote the agenda of the kingdom of darkness have been able to deceive people in this nation and around the world into believing it's fine to identify as a cat, a dog, a humanoid, or a gender other than the one God created you as; to have abortion after abortion; to get married and divorced over and over again for frivolous reasons; and to sleep around and still preach from the pulpit on Sundays. You can be gay, transgender, or nonbinary, and you can watch as much violence and perversion as your flesh wants. Do what thou wilt.

Members of the media and activist groups who serve the same ancient demons as Crowley, Egypt, and Rome, as well as so-called churches, have brought down the temperature of the Word of God to lukewarm. They have theologically manipulated the Word, taking every foul maggot and uncleanness and mashing them up until they look similar to something spiritually edible. And they have welcomed to the pulpit every serpent who wants to slither in and share. As a result, the church now has deceived masses of lost sheep who think they can do whatever they want and God will just accept it. There is no accountability, no culpability, no responsibility, and no consequences for lusts of the flesh, sinful behavior, and downright rebellion against God and His Word. The verse "There is therefore now no condemnation to those who are in Christ Jesus" (Rom. 8:1, NKJV) has been rewritten to mean "Do what thou wilt shall be the whole of the Law."

That is *not* what that means.

The rest of the verse reads, "who do not walk according to the flesh, but according to the Spirit." The enemy is taking a little bit of truth and mixing it with a whole lot of lie.

There are accounts in the Gospels of times when Jesus did not condemn; however, He has a standard. He expects the ones He is not condemning to come under that standard. In fact, He said, "Go and sin no more" (John 8:11, NKJV). John 5:14 says, "Afterward Jesus found [the man healed at the pool of Bethesda] in the temple and said to him, 'Behold, you have become well; do not sin anymore, so that nothing worse happens to you'" (NASB).

This fact about Jesus' exchange with a man He healed has been stripped from many pulpits in the churches today as varnish off a footlocker! There are no boundaries and no accountability for sin—and I'm talking about outright, continual, rebellious sin, not those who are struggling and trying to become stronger in the Lord. This has occurred because of an idea connected to "Do what thou wilt." It seems innocent on the outside, but it is toxic on the inside, and the kingdom of darkness has turned the volume up to full blast on the idea. It is called tolerance.

Tolerance

Merriam-Webster defines *tolerance* as "sympathy or indulgence for beliefs or practices differing from or conflicting with one's own; the act of allowing something; the allowable deviation from a standard."[16] *Indulge* means "to yield to the desire of; to treat with excessive leniency, generosity, or consideration; to give free rein to."[17]

So *tolerance* is excessive indulgence of a desire. The problem is when something is dysfunctional, dark, and damaging at its core and that something is excessively indulged, it enables a beast with an insatiable appetite for destruction. Tolerance and enabling go hand in hand. Tolerance almost never builds character—it destroys it. It keeps in bondage those who have given themselves over to such sin. It keeps man in chains rather than in the freedom found through Christ.

The enemy then utilizes the one in bondage as a slave to put chains on others as well. Tolerance is a breeding ground for entitlement, perverse behavior, pride, and rebellion. Again, the Word of God says, "Rebellion is as the sin of witchcraft" (1 Sam. 15:23, NKJV). Rebellions are not tolerated by God; they are put down.

The colosseum of media and technology has packaged tolerance as something humane, loving, and noble when in fact it is a vicious root from which the offshoot is venom. Love and tolerance are two very different things. To tolerate is to enable destructive behaviors to continue. To love is to speak the truth, to share the transforming love we experience through Christ, and to bring freedom to the captives by helping them purge what is invasive and damaging in their lives.

The standard of love stays steady no matter the tantrums, threats, or shouts. The standard of love does not yield to the angry crowd. Instead, the standard of love encourages people to come in line with the standard and to be transformed by it. It brings freedom, not bondage. It comes with respect. It comes with boundaries, something the media more and more have attempted to make obsolete because pride and tolerance feed their dark agenda.

The world says *love* means being able to do whatever you want, to feed all the lusts of your flesh, and to seek only your own pleasure. But that is not the truth. The truth is this:

> Love endures with patience and serenity, love is kind
> and thoughtful, and is not jealous or envious; love does
> not brag and is not proud or arrogant. It is not rude; it
> is not self-seeking, it is not provoked [nor overly sensi-
> tive and easily angered]; it does not take into account

a wrong endured. It does not rejoice at injustice, but
rejoices with the truth [when right and truth prevail].
—1 CORINTHIANS 13:4–6

Nowhere in this scripture does it say love enables, love tol-
erates bad behavior, love succumbs to abusive demands, love
permits what feels right, and love breaks His laws. Nowhere
does this scripture imply any of this; however, the corrupt
shepherds, the showmen, and the false prophets would have
you believe it. That is why, as I have said many times in this
book, you must know the truth to recognize what is false.
You must know the Word of God so you can discern the
deception and avoid the tactics of the enemy.

CHAPTER 8

THE SHEPHERDS AND THE SHOWMEN

THERE IS A battle of the revelationary war being fought on the soil of the church, one that has intensified over the past six years. This has impacted the body of Christ across multiple factions and has involved multiple continents. This battle within the revelationary war is dropping one of the greatest plumb lines and measuring rods in history on the leaders of the church.

On January 18, 2021, I released a teaching called "The Truth About Ministry and Its Options in America." Here is an excerpt from this teaching:

> The Lord is making a serious adjustment in this country right now. As a chiropractor adjusts and you hear the cracks and the noise, so shall it be now. The Lord is dropping a plumbline, a measuring rod. There are two camps.
>
> Camp 1 is more concerned about enabling people's feelings, keeping them happy by telling them exactly what they want to hear. Out of fear of losing what these leaders have built, they are recanting what God says in His Word. Out of peer pressure they are appeasing people because they fear the people.

They are those who are concerned about the superficial and keeping everything on the surface to appease the masses.

Mega churches, mega platforms, and mega personalities, when unchecked and [led] by one drinking from a tainted well, easily become a megaphone for an Operation Mockingbird type of strategy to enter the church and become the peddler of genetically engineered seed that grows as an invasive vine and ensnares the lives of the sheep.

Camp 2 is those who are standing firmly in what *the Lord* said, refusing to back down, fearing God more than man.

They are those who are marching ahead, getting bolder in the Lord.

They are those concerned about watching over the promise to its completion.

The *showmen* are in camp 1, and the *shepherds* are in camp 2.

Though they may appear in ways similar, standing at the pulpit or speaking online, their foundations and motives are *very* different.

Here is a word from the Lord I released on May 17, 2021:

The plumb line has been dropped. The measuring rod for leadership and the churches for judgment begins in the house of God, and I, the Lord, shall now expose the most shocking coverups amongst leadership who wanted to toy with ungodly principles and mammon and other gods and do what they were instructed. For an unholy cord binds them to the corrupt, and now I, the Lord, shall cut that cord and *prune*. For the leadership who stands in this hour, I, the Lord, *will* protect, and I will prosper and excel them in the midst of the pressure and the shaking. I shall steady them upon the solid rock of *My Son* Yeshua, Jesus, who died for your sins.

And the Spirit of the Lord says this day, the true men and women behind the mask will be exposed in this hour. I am pressing it forth and laying it plainly before the people, for this is the time to choose this day whom you will serve. Who will you serve, oh America, with your amber waves of grain? Oh, I speak to the eagle. I speak to the eagle, and I speak life and praise into its wings, and it shall lift its wings and glorify the God in heaven who is warring on your behalf.

Here is an excerpt from a word from the Lord I released December 14, 2022:

Those who have sown embellishments and greed and what comes from the flesh shall reap stubble in this hour, dry stubble. There shall be no fruit that is beared forth from the actions of those who have comingled the darkness with the light, who have comingled wheat and tares, who have comingled resources and funds, and who have comingled the things of the flesh with the holy things of God. I, the Lord thy God, am dropping a plumbline in this hour, and it shall be divided. *Yes*, it shall be divided, says the Lord. The rod of correction has gone forth from *My* throne, says the Lord, as well as promotion. Correction and promotion in this hour—this you shall see, says the Lord. I chastise those I love, says the Lord. However, I also bring justification and rectification to what has been done to *My* children to harm, sabotage, hurt the path I have put them on. You shall see an abrupt stop be put to such, says the Lord in this hour.

Here is a word from the Lord I released on March 17, 2023:

> Do not allow the enemy, the father of lies, to veer you.
> For many who claim to be serving me and doing such
> for My name are nothing more than self-glorified "war
> heroes" and kings of a hill of their own making. That
> has little to do with serving Me and much to do with
> serving themselves, says the Lord. They are serving
> *themselves*. What they have amassed was not of Me; it
> was of man. And that plumbline is being dropped in
> this hour.

THE PLUMB LINE

A plumb line is a measuring rod, a standard. Amos 7:7–8
(NKJV) says,

> Thus He showed me: Behold, the Lord stood on a wall
> made with a plumb line, with a plumb line in His hand.
> And the LORD said to me, "Amos, what do you see?"
> And I said, "A plumb line."
> Then the Lord said: "Behold, I am setting a plumb
> line in the midst of My people Israel."

The Lord is setting up a plumb line between the shepherds and the showmen in this hour. The showmen are the ones putting on a superficial show rather than preaching and teaching the truth. The showmen are the ones who are giving in to peer pressure and pressure from society. They are giving in to the fear of man. They are false prophets, sowing invasive weeds in the church.

The shepherds have the belt of truth fastened firmly around their waists. They are preaching and teaching the truth. They stand firmly on the truth of the Word of God.

They fear God, not man. They are true prophets, true five-fold ministers, sowing seeds of truth and faith in the church.

The showmen and Simon the sorcerer (from the Book of Acts) have some unique similarities. The account of Philip (a shepherd) and Simon the sorcerer (a showman) unfolds this way:

> Now there was a man named Simon, who formerly was practicing magic in the city and astonishing the people of Samaria, *claiming to be someone great*; and they all, from smallest to greatest, *were giving attention to him*, saying, "This man is what is called the Great Power of God."
>
> —ACTS 8:9–10, NASB, EMPHASIS ADDED

Simon was claiming to be someone great. And because of that claim, he was getting a lot of attention. This is a key principle to understand. God's power, authority, and favor working through Simon was *not* what promoted Simon. It was *not* what went before Simon. Instead, it was his self-promotion, his act of smoke and mirrors, and *his* claims he was someone great that he planted among the people. He was counterfeit, packaged to look similar to the "Great Power of God" when it was really nothing more than an empty illusion for people who lacked discernment.

The people did not have a measuring rod to test Simon's act against. Simon was trying to make things happen, to put forth an image that he was somebody with a great power. Pride and flesh were leading around Simon by the neck. And in turn Simon was distracting the people and feeding them a deception, a false reality, sour milk. It was nothing nourishing, nothing that would cause those people to turn to the Lord. Instead, they were turning to Simon.

The account continues,

> And they were giving him attention because he had for
> a long time astonished them with his magic arts. But
> when they believed Philip preaching the good news
> about the kingdom of God and the name of Jesus Christ,
> they were being baptized, men and women alike. Even
> Simon himself believed; and after being baptized, he
> continued on with Philip, and as he observed signs and
> great miracles taking place, he was constantly amazed.
> —ACTS 8:11–13, NASB

The illusion, the show, was getting the attention until the
but entered: "But when they *believed* Philip…" Enter Philip,
a disciple and shepherd who was filled with the Holy Spirit.
This is where the plumb line was dropped right before the
people. It was the true power of God with one who truly
operated in it contending against the power of illusion. When
Philip and the power of God entered that area, the people
not only saw the difference but also felt it. The true transforming power of God will always expose the dark illusions
and deceptions that give the appearance of an unadulterated
power but that carry motives to distract and lead astray.

> Now when the apostles in Jerusalem heard that
> Samaria had received the word of God, they sent them
> Peter and John, who came down and prayed for them
> that they might receive the Holy Spirit. For He had not
> yet fallen upon any of them; they had simply been bap-
> tized in the name of the Lord Jesus. Then they began
> laying their hands on them, and they were receiving
> the Holy Spirit.
> —ACTS 8:14–17, NASB

The Holy Spirit, the Ruach HaKodesh, is the Counselor. A counselor worth their salt, for we are the salt of the earth (Matt. 5:13), will help guide you out of darkness into all truth and equip you to see through a discerning lens so what is hidden is exposed and dealt with. We are bought with the highest price ever paid, the blood of Jesus Christ shed on the cross, and there is nothing we could ever do, no amount of money we could ever pay, for such a price. The Holy Spirit bears witness to this in our lives.

THE SHOWMEN

The account of Simon the sorcerer in Acts continues,

> Now when Simon saw that the Spirit was bestowed through the laying on of the apostles' hands, he offered them money, saying, "Give this authority to me as well, so that everyone on whom I lay my hands may receive the Holy Spirit."
>
> —ACTS 8:18–19, NASB

This is so important. Simon offered the disciples money he gained by deceiving the people through magic and the illusion that he had a power from God that he never had. He was attempting to buy the power of God with defiled tender.

This was not about giving unto the Lord freely and cheerfully. No, this was the lust of the flesh, with Simon coveting a power far greater than his act and attempting to transactionally take possession of a gift. The disciples were called to their positions, but Simon was attempting to buy his way into such a position, to take possession of a power that would have deceived the people into believing Simon's magic arts truly came from the Lord. From Simon's perspective this would have solidified that status. It also would have caused his many prior deceptions to be validated. It would have ratified corrupt actions as upright.

Simon was attempting to make things happen on his own to present an anointing he did not possess. This at its core is the driving motive of a showman. The want is to cause the perception that they possess power, authority, and anointing from God, but it is all appearance and no substance—it's a superficial show. They entertain rather than enlighten through and by the Word of God. Simon the sorcerer was just an entertainer, an entertainer who enticed the people, mesmerizing them with a spectacle and causing many to put their faith in a power of which the source was a complete fabrication. Fabrications lead to fallacies that lead to falls and treacherous paths for those who believe the showman, for showmen lead the people into weeds and thorns, not green pastures.

> But Peter said to him, "May your silver perish with you, because you thought you could obtain the gift of God with money! You have no part or portion in this matter, for your heart is not right before God."
>
> —Acts 8:20–21, NASB

This is a loaded statement and alludes to an event in the Old Testament. Zechariah 11:10–17 (NASB, emphasis added) says,

> I took my staff Favor and cut it in pieces, to break my covenant which I had made with all the peoples. So it was broken on that day, and thus the afflicted of the flock who were watching me realized that it was the word of the LORD. I said to them, "If it is good in your sight, give me my wages; but if not, never mind!" So *they weighed out thirty shekels of silver as my wages.* Then the LORD said to me, "Throw it to the potter, that magnificent price at which I was valued by them." So I

took the thirty shekels of silver and threw them to the potter in the house of the LORD. Then I cut in pieces my second staff Union, to break the brotherhood between Judah and Israel.

The LORD said to me, "Take again for yourself the equipment of a foolish shepherd. For behold, I am going to raise up a shepherd in the land who will not care for the perishing, seek the scattered, heal the broken, or sustain the one standing, but will devour the flesh of the fat sheep and tear off their hoofs. Woe to the worthless shepherd who leaves the flock! A sword will be on his arm and on his right eye! His arm will be totally withered and his right eye will be blind."

Foolish shepherds are the showmen. They care more about appearance and how it looks rather than truly shepherding and teaching the flock. The Lord makes it very clear here how He feels about such worthless shepherds and what happens to them. Also, in this case silver was used to try to undermine the true power of God and the Word of the Lord, so keep that in mind. The Lord told Zechariah to go throw that silver to the potter for its *magnificent price*, a blatantly sarcastic comment, because it was truly an insult, the thirty pieces of silver. This ties to the Book of Matthew, which ties to the showdown between Peter the shepherd and Simon, a showman.

Then one of the twelve, called Judas Iscariot, went to the chief priests and said, "What are you willing to give me if I deliver Him to you?" And they counted out to him thirty pieces of silver. So from that time he sought opportunity to betray Him.

—MATTHEW 26:14–16, NKJV

119

The driving forces of the betrayal were money and greed. First Timothy 6:10 says, "For the love of money is a root of all sorts of evil, and some by longing for it have wandered away from the faith and pierced themselves with many griefs" (NASB).

"Thirty pieces of silver," a *magnificent price*. The Lord and His Word were once again undermined by a transactional change having to do with power. Either gaining power or stopping it was involved in all these cases with a transaction. The result of such betrayal is in Matthew 27:3–8 (NKJV):

> Then Judas, His betrayer, seeing that He had been condemned, was remorseful and brought back the thirty pieces of silver to the chief priests and elders, saying, "I have sinned by betraying innocent blood."
>
> And they said, "What is that to us? You see to it!"
>
> Then he threw down the pieces of silver in the temple and departed, and went and hanged himself.
>
> But the chief priests took the silver pieces and said, "It is not lawful to put them into the treasury, because they are the price of blood." And they consulted together and bought with them the potter's field, to bury strangers in. Therefore that field has been called the Field of Blood to this day.

That silver perished with Judas because the field where he died was bought with those thirty pieces of silver.

Judas took the silver and threw it down in the temple, just as Zechariah threw silver in the potter's house. Judas took his own life after what he had done, his deep level of betrayal against Jesus and helping a bunch of corrupt showmen, the Pharisees, take down and destroy the true power of God they did not possess. Showmen harbor much envy against shepherds.

The Pharisees were showmen and exhibitionists with all the required pomp and circumstance. They had the appearance and the show of holiness and righteousness, when they really were whitewashed tombs. They looked the part but had no power or authority to operate in the true power of God. Jesus' teaching, healing, delivering, and setting free captives truly exposed their hidden agenda. A plumb line was dropped when Jesus' ministry began.

WATERED DOWN

The Pharisees were all show, all appearance, and superficial, with zero interest in truly shepherding the people. In fact, they looked down on the people and saw them as means to their end. They reveled in all the attention they received, the perks they accessed by working with the Roman governing body, the false authority they walked in, and the illusion of holiness, when really they emitted a pious stench. Much of who they were was smoke and mirrors. Did you ever wonder how they caught the woman in the act of adultery and threw her before Jesus if none of them was in the room?

Back to Simon the sorcerer's story. Again,

> Peter said to him, "May your silver perish with you, because you thought you could obtain the gift of God with money! You have no part or portion in this matter, for your heart is not right before God."
>
> —ACTS 8:20–21, NASB

"May your silver perish with you." This is what happened in the Book of Zechariah and what happened with Judas in the Gospel of Matthew, and here Peter boldly says the same to Simon because the motive of Simon's heart was tainted. Simon's desire for power was corrupted, and he attempted to buy the anointing, to purchase the power of God, given through Christ Jesus' death on the cross to those who come to the Lord with a humble heart and contrite spirit.

This is what happens with showmen. They attempt to purchase the anointing and market it to benefit only themselves. Today, there are showmen who use marketing agencies, publicists, and advertisers to make them appear more powerful, knowledgeable, and anointed than they really are. In fact, many times these showmen will strip the anointing off a ministry as, again, varnish off a footlocker because the world understands only its own business. The world does not have any wisdom about how to handle the Lord's matters and business.

When showmen are in the pulpit, theology and the Word of God become more and more watered down. Believers become lukewarm. Scripture is twisted or ignored, and every serpent with an agenda is welcomed in to change ministries at their foundations. These serpents possess a power that is packaged as opening doors of opportunity to the ministry, giving it a larger arena and reach. However, the cost is handing Jesus over to the Pharisees and doing away with everything transforming and convicting about the Word. Suddenly, adultery, abortion, gay marriage, and a host of hot-button issues receive advocacy from the showmen.

A shepherd has a firm biblical standard. All are welcome to come to church and hear the good news; however, there is a firm biblical standard, and it will not be changed to keep anyone comfortable in their sin! It will not be changed to grant permission to continue in the sin.

Showmen give the public perception that God condones and allows things His Word says clearly He does not. Showmen water down the Word to reach a greater audience and open doors with the upper-echelon crowd that will help make things happen for them. They are looking to the world for promotion. But when it comes to true promotion in ministry, in the church, the world has nothing to do with it. The Lord is the One who promotes.

Showmen end up drawing in the people by preaching and teaching what those people want to hear, catering to their emotions. Feeding people such a meal all the time is like giving only sour milk and candy to children. It is going to stunt their growth and make them very sick. Nothing will function the way it should in their lives. Showmen stunt the growth of the sheep, preventing them from maturing spiritually in the Lord.

Back to the story.

> [Peter said,] "Therefore repent of this wickedness of yours, and pray the Lord that, if possible, the intention of your heart may be forgiven you. For I see that you are in the gall of bitterness and in the bondage of iniquity." But Simon answered and said, "Pray to the Lord for me yourselves, so that nothing of what you have said may come upon me."
>
> —ACTS 8:22–24, NASB

In Galatians 5:19–21 (NKJV) the apostle Paul warned about the works of the flesh:

> Now the works of the flesh are evident, which are: adultery, fornication, uncleanness, lewdness, idolatry, sorcery, hatred, contentions, jealousies, outbursts of wrath, selfish ambitions, dissensions, heresies, envy, murders, drunkenness, revelries, and the like; of which I tell you beforehand, just as I also told you in time past, that those who practice such things will not inherit the kingdom of God.

This is exactly what Simon the sorcerer did, and it is exactly what the showmen engage in that ultimately ends up pulling the curtain back on their "great and powerful" personas.

At the end of the movie *The Wizard of Oz*, Dorothy, Scarecrow, Tin Man, and Cowardly Lion (which is exactly what Satan is, by the way) finally go before the "great and powerful" Oz to ask for what they need, but the wizard is a showman and cannot fulfill their needs, because he has no real power. Oz had fabricated who he truly was.

When Oz rejects their petitions, Dorothy's little dog, Toto, runs to a curtain, latches on to it with his teeth, and pulls it back to expose who Oz truly is—nothing more than a feeble old man pretending to be a great and powerful being. All his power was generated with a hologram machine. No true power to help people existed. Toto is an example of the foolish things of this world being used to confound the wise. No one ever expected a little dog would bring down the whole operation in Emerald City, just as no one expected a teenage shepherd boy named David to kill a nine-foot-tall war champion with a slingshot and a stone.

It's time to pull back the curtain on the showmen who are watering down the truth of the Word and stunting the spiritual growth of believers. It's time for the shepherds to stand up.

BEING A SHEPHERD

On one side of the plumb line are the showmen, the false prophets deceiving people by watering down and twisting the Word of God. On the other side of the plumb line are the shepherds.

Psalm 23:1 says, "The LORD is my shepherd; I shall not want" (NKJV). To explain what shepherds truly are, I am going to share with you something the Lord taught me in my own life.

At Ark of Grace Sanctuary I have two sheep, Archie and Moses. When they came to be residents here at the Ark, the Lord said to me, "I am going to teach you firsthand why I call My people sheep." Oh boy, was I in for it.

Archie escaped a farm in Georgia as a baby, and by the hand of God he survived the backwoods and was found very close to Passover by a family when he wandered onto their property. They kept him for a while when he was a baby; however, the time came when he was growing and needed a permanent place, so they asked us to take him. Archie was my first, and he has a personality. If you touch him and he is not in the mood, he will headbutt you. Much more caution must be used with Archie, but once he warms up to you, he can be quite agreeable.

Moses is our Passover baby. Two years ago he was born on a local farm during Passover. His mother rejected him, and the owner of the farm found him half dead and intervened with lifesaving measures. Moses needed a lot of care, so he was brought to us. Moses lived in our home the first four months of his life. Our dog Missy mothered him, and Moses thought he was a dog there for a while, not a sheep—kind of as the biblical Moses thought he was an Egyptian for a while, not a Jew.

This was my Psalm 23 experience, learning what a shepherd is. What I learned through both Moses and Archie translates to the church and the shepherds.

First of all, sheep have very little defense without their shepherd. The shepherd is their defense against danger and predators. The shepherd looks out ahead and sees danger coming before the sheep know it's there. The shepherd is there to keep the sheep in nourishing, good pastures and to not allow them to wander. Sheep have little sense, and if left to their own devices, they can enter dangerous territory.

Sheep need a very specific diet, and if they are not fed properly, they can develop severe health issues, including stones in their bladders, which can cause a life-threatening blockage.

Sheep can get very worked up and agitated if something is not right in their environment or if something has been allowed in that is unfamiliar to them. Sometimes because they cannot reason what the source is, they may try to take that agitation out on the shepherd.

Sheep know the voice of their shepherd. John 10:27–28 says, "My sheep hear My voice, and I know them, and they follow Me; and I give eternal life to them, and they will never perish; and no one will snatch them out of My hand" (NASB). Moses and Archie both know my voice. Moses sees me, and he runs to me; I call to him, and he calls back. Jeremiah 33:3 says, "Call to Me and I will answer you, and I will tell you great and mighty things, which you do not know" (NASB).

Sheep pens can be very dirty, and they need to be kept clean. Otherwise, the door is opened for illness and for invasive weeds that do not belong to grow. The sheep, as their wool grows, must be sheared. This especially applies in the warmer weather, to protect them. This is all the responsibility of the shepherd.

Sheep can get stressed easily, and stress can be toxic to sheep. They do have a fight-or-flight mechanism when something has gone awry with them. Sheep are not completely dumb; however, they are overly curious and want to consume *everything* they shouldn't. They can be strong-willed, and if not given boundaries, they will challenge quite a bit. This is especially true of the rams, the male sheep.

Sheep need boundaries from the shepherd and to understand the shepherd is the one leading. Boundaries protect sheep from predators, from bodily harm, and from fighting with each other. The shepherd establishes the boundaries, and the sheep must come in line. In fact, when a sheep within the flock continues to challenge the shepherd—and what I am about to tell you, I had to do to Moses when he was about eight months old or so—the shepherd must take the sheep, pin it to the ground, and hold it there until it stops struggling. This very clearly signals to the sheep that the shepherd is much stronger than it is.

This is important in the world of livestock because there is an alpha system. One sheep or one pig or one goat submits to the other because they understand that physically, they are weaker than the other sheep or pig or goat. The same concept applies with the shepherd. The sheep must be held in place until it stops struggling so it experiences the dominance and authority of the shepherd. When the sheep stops struggling, the shepherd can let the sheep up, and the sheep will indeed submit. Because sheep are herd animals, they tend to follow each other. So when the alpha sheep submits, the rest will follow suit and submit to the shepherd.

When sheep find themselves in danger, it is the shepherd that steps in to rescue them. It is the covering and strength of the shepherd that keep the sheep from harm, which means shepherds at times must engage with predators attempting to harm the flock, fight them off, and cause them to flee from the area. Shepherds do not welcome in wolves, lions, bears, or any other predator to just ravage their flock. They eliminate the threat. A threat can send a flock into complete confusion and panic, which can oftentimes give predators the upper hand to steal what does not belong to them. The shepherd maintains order and knows exactly what to do when danger attempts to approach. From personal experience I have gone tearing outside at 2:00 a.m. in my bathrobe because I heard a pack of coyotes a little too close to where Archie and Moses were. I will go out during the night and chase off predators. I do not leave it to chance. I hold my position and defend the flock because I am their shepherd.

Will the Real Shepherds Please Stand Up?

A shepherd must be a leader, not an entertainer. Experience is one of the best teachers when it comes to leading. Shepherds must guard and care for the flock God has given them the same way I guard and care for Archie and Moses.

"The Lord is my shepherd; I shall not want" (Ps. 23:1, nkjv). The sheep do not want because they are fed properly by the shepherd and given appropriate cover and boundaries. The sheep do not want to stray to try to find what they think they are missing.

"He makes me lie down in green pastures; He leads me beside quiet waters. He restores my soul; He guides me in the paths of righteousness for His name's sake" (Ps. 23:2–3, nasb). The shepherd leads, restores, and guides in paths of righteousness. A good shepherd does not lead the flock down a path of folly or delusion or deception but one of uprightness and maturity and truth. A good shepherd challenges the sheep when immature behavior rears up and deals with the one who has the potential to taint the flock.

In Galatians 5:22–23 the fruits of the spirit are presented: "But the fruit of the Spirit is love, joy, peace, longsuffering, kindness, goodness, faithfulness, gentleness, self-control. Against such there is no law" (nkjv). Not only do true shepherds bear this fruit in their lives, but they also make the conditions right for the flock to bear fruit in their lives. They do this by maintaining a solid biblical standard that is not lowered for the sheep to stay nice and comfortable in their sin. The standard is maintained, challenging the sheep to mature, which then helps them bear fruit. The pastors and prophets—actually anyone in the fivefold ministry—should be staunch in their resolve in the culture and environment we find ourselves in at present.

We have an epidemic today of Bible colleges bringing in young men and women and trying to make them fit the mold of a shepherd when they were not created to be such and are often too young. David slew Goliath as a teenager, but he did not become king for another fifteen years, after the Lord took him through a wilderness experience. Much of the younger generation has not been through the experiences they would need to successfully pastor a congregation. A three- or four-year program with no real-life experience does not give pastors the foundation, the experience, or the emotional maturity they need to lead. If they are sent into this ravenous world unprepared and too young and then given a flock, the majority of those unprepared pastors are going to impact that flock not for the better.

Too many of the younger generation of pastors today want to circumvent the process of maturing in the Lord altogether. They are often placed in leadership while they are still thinking like teenagers, their convictions are still somewhat superficial, and they are blown around with every wind of doctrine and popular cause. They join the ranks of the showmen and sell out to wokeism, perversion, and so on.

Showmen rewrite or twist the Word of God to make acceptable the things they sold out to. They manipulate scriptures to make rebellion acceptable. Rather than a shepherd, they become a publicist God never wanted, putting a spin on deception to make it seem like the truth. Believers are meant to have boundaries and be deeply convicted by the Word of God, but that won't happen if shepherds are turning into showmen and trying to make the Word of God socially acceptable and digestible to the masses. The showmen are putting the sheep on a road of perdition that leads to bondage, confusion, anxiety, anger, doubt, and a lack of discipline and emotional maturity.

Showmen have caused the sheep to believe that Jesus was and is a pushover and that almighty God is just a harmless, cute kitten. He is the Lion of Judah—let us not forget! The showmen have stripped the fear of and reverence for God from the flock. Proverbs 9:10 says, "The fear of the LORD is the beginning of wisdom, and the knowledge of the Holy One is understanding" (NKJV). The goal of the wolves and serpents is to get the shepherd to raise a false standard, speak a false word, and preach an alternative gospel so the deceptive air of credibility is presented before the people.

Shepherds are meant to be steadfast with biblical standards, not lowering them for sheep who throw tantrums or wolves who manipulate the flock or serpents who slither in with very tempting pieces of fruit. In this day and age if you stand for nothing, you will indeed fall for everything and become a schizophrenic voice for the almost daily-changing agendas.

The world of social media has added another problematic layer to being able to effectively shepherd the flock. The sheep biting and the wolves attacking can now remain faceless with nothing more than a fake screen name and an avatar. Wolves generally hunt in packs and try to surround their prey. There is a faction of those wolves called trolls and bots; they attack and apply pressure to overwhelm shepherds so they will put down their staffs and stop their defense of the gospel of Jesus Christ. The attack can be overwhelming as they try to force shepherds to change their standards and change their message to accommodate the agendas of the kingdom of darkness.

At their core these are *not* political issues we face. These are biblical issues that modern-day spin doctors working on behalf of the enemy have turned into political issues to divide the body of Christ and deceive shepherds into becoming showmen. The enemy knows there is much power in agreement, which is why one of his tactics is to cause division.

The agenda of the kingdom of darkness has caused the church to face off against itself, but it has revealed who the true shepherds are—the ones who face the wolves, the lions, the serpents, the trolls—and stand their ground with the belt of truth tied firmly around their waists. James 4:7 states, "Therefore submit to God. Resist the devil and he will flee from you" (NKJV).

In an hour of Simon the sorcerers and superficial showmen, will the real shepherds please stand up?

This is the time to truly get in that field and defend the faith and the flock, to have the true courage of your convictions, and to refuse to sell out God for a watered-down Word that doesn't nourish and that makes the soul sick. We face a dark forest of wicked agendas and an arena of digital wolves and serpents looking to destroy flocks, take down shepherds, and weaken the biblical foundation of the church that has endured through time. Joshua 23:10 says, "One man of you shall chase a thousand, for the LORD your God is He who fights for you, as He promised you" (NKJV).

An excerpt from a word from the Lord I delivered on May 24, 2021, states:

> And says the Spirit of the Lord this day, I, the Lord, am constructing a new foundation in the church. From the ash and the persecution and the threats, a church is arising who has a boldness and a desire to truly shepherd, to truly stand for *My* Word; a church arising with a new breed of leadership, who do not just speak as soothsayers, manipulators, or will only go so far and

box themselves in. No, this is a new breed of leadership, says the Lord, those who have been refined, who have stood in the heat boldly in their faith and have come out victorious, says the Lord of Hosts.

Armor up, according to Ephesians 6. Pick up that shepherding staff and defend the flock and the faith, knowing the Lord is with you. It is time for this dark advance to be forced to retreat by the power and authority given to us through Christ Jesus. Almighty God is our *Khatan*.

In *The Book of Mysteries*, Jonathan Cahn writes,

Khatan means the bridegroom, but it goes deeper than that. It can be translated as he who joins himself....Most people see God as distant, unapproachable, One we must convince to forgive us. Most religions are based on that...on all we have to do to get God to accept us. But the truth is radically different. God is the Khatan. So it is He who wills to join Himself to you. It is His nature, His heart, and His desire to join His life to yours. You don't have to convince Him to love you—He already does. The Khatan is love... the One who becomes one with you. It is not you who must approach Him....It is He who approaches you. And in the mystery of the Khatan is the mystery of everything...the mystery of salvation. It is because God is the Khatan that He has joined Himself to us. He has joined all that is Him to all that is you. So there's no part of you that He will not join Himself to...no matter how dark it is, no matter how sinful, no matter how ungodly. Because He is the Khatan, He even joined Himself to your sins. What is the death of Messiah on the cross? It is the Khatan...He who joins Himself, joining Himself to everything you are, even and especially to the most ungodly parts of your life. And because of this miracle, there is now nothing that can separate you anymore from His love.[1]

What the true shepherds and the nation need to take hold of in this time is the Khatan—the Lord joining Himself to all that is us. In every step taken and every breath that is breathed, we need the Khatan. Now more than ever leadership must be joined in this deep way to the Lord. The Khatan joins to our souls.

Our nation has a soul, and many things have joined to it to put it in chains, to put America in graveclothes. There is a battle utilizing the revelatory power of almighty God to fight against the deception of the enemy so that the nation can come forth out of the dark place it was lured into. It is the battle for the soul of the nation.

CHAPTER 9

A SPIRITUAL CYCLE: COVENANT TO REBELLION

I N A POWERFUL writing from 1954, evangelist Billy Graham said:

> A war of ideologies is being waged throughout the world, a war of the secular against the spiritual. The actual battles in the areas of combat are only material manifestations of the larger battle that rages in the hearts of men throughout the earth. Will it be truth or a lie? Will we be motivated by materialistic philosophy or spiritual power? Will we be led by Jehovah God—or duped by Satan? The battle lines are clearly drawn.[1]

We really are in a war of ideologies, a war between the truth and lies.

The battle is part of a long-term spiritual war, as well as a spiritual cycle. Just as the history of the Jewish people started with a covenant and then they went through repeated cycles of rebellion and judgment, repentance and revival, so the history of the US started with covenant, followed by periods of rebellion and judgment, repentance and revival. As believers we need to recognize the spiritual cycle so we can defend against the tactics of the enemy.

The enemy has been looking for open and unattended avenues to attack and take territory since the forming of this nation in 1776. It is part of the spiritual cycle—he wants to push toward rebellion and judgment. During the Revolutionary War the victory of the colonists, led by Gen. George Washington and with the providence and protection of almighty God, was a major blow to the enemy's territories and interests. It was a blow to tyranny, and it opened a locked gate to freedom. Freedom from tyranny meant people were free to worship the Lord in spirit and in truth. It meant a foundation of morality, family, reverence for our Creator, and truth could be set in place and built upon. The wise man builds His house upon the rock (Matt. 7:24).

THE COVENANT

The Declaration of Independence upon which our freedom as a nation was built was signed and sealed. Here is a crucial excerpt:

> We hold these truths to be self-evident, that all men are created equal, that they are endowed by their Creator with certain unalienable Rights, that among these are Life, Liberty and the pursuit of Happiness. That to secure these rights, Governments are instituted among Men, deriving their just powers from the consent of the governed. That whenever any Form of Government becomes destructive of these ends, it is the Right of the People to alter or to abolish it, and to institute new Government, laying its foundation on such principles and organizing its powers in such form,

as to them shall seem most likely to effect their Safety and Happiness.[2]

On April 30, 1789, thirteen years after the Declaration of Independence was signed, George Washington made a covenant with almighty God during his first inauguration, at Federal Hall in New York City.

I was birthed into this world at Einstein Hospital in the Bronx, New York—it is the territory in which the Lord raised me up. Do you ever wonder why the enemy built up New York City with such extreme liberalism? Well, I think it was because it was the very soil in which Washington's covenant was made. The enemy then went to work, diligently building up much corruption, perversion, and godlessness upon that soil. This will come into play as we continue.

When George Washington took the oath of office at Federal Hall in New York City, the Bible used was open to Genesis 49, which begins, "And Jacob called unto his sons, and said, Gather yourselves together, that I may tell you that which shall befall you in the last days" (Gen. 49:1, KJV). After Washington took the oath, he bent over the Word of God and kissed it in an act of reverence to His God, the One who had delivered him from the snare of the fowler so many times before.

Washington made a covenant between the nation and God and stated that no nation could expect to be blessed by the Lord if they turn away from Him, that if a nation forgets almighty God, they shall lose the blessing that God has bestowed upon them.

Many prophets in the Bible warned the nation of Israel in a similar way. Ezekiel, Jeremiah, Hosea, and Elijah, among others, were prophets during times when there were rebellious kings leading Israel toward an abyss of judgment. The United States and Israel are connected by a vein in the spirit, and because of this events within one nation often have parallels in the other.

RESULTS OF REBELLION

The rebellion of Israel against almighty God, His Word, and His covenant caused the Lord to take His hand of protection off Israel. Because of their rebellion and their turn to satanic and pagan worship and rules of law, judgment came. Israel was ravaged by foreign armies and endured drought, famine, and pestilence. Similar things have occurred in the United States of America.

The covenant made on April 30, 1789, was made in the area that is now called Ground Zero. Federal Hall is only about a mile from the World Trade Center, where on September 11, 2001, the nation and the world witnessed the destruction of the Twin Towers. I was working as an accountant at a commodities trading firm in Stamford, Connecticut, and we were evacuated and sent home.

Our nation's leaders, from the mayor of New York to the president, vowed, "We will rebuild."[3] Mentally take note of the three-word slogan, for a pattern will emerge with this as we go further. In making such a declaration, the nation not only ultimately turned from God but stood in rebellion challenging Him.

Isaiah 9:10–11 says, "'The bricks have fallen down, but we will rebuild with hewn stones; the *sycamores* are cut down, but we will replace them with *cedars*.' Therefore the Lord shall set up the adversaries of Rezin against him, and spur his enemies on" (NKJV, emphasis added). The verse is about judgment on the people of Israel, but the purpose of that judgment was restoration—God wanted His people to repent.

But they didn't; instead, they responded with defiance, with continued rebellion: "We will rebuild."

On September 11, 2001, God called the people of America to repent. He wanted restoration and revival. But although churches were filled up in the weeks following the attack, there was no repentance, there was no return to the Lord, and there was no revival. As a nation, the response was defiance and continued rebellion.

St. Paul's Chapel, where George Washington prayed to God on the day of his inauguration, was protected on 9/11 by a sycamore tree that was destroyed by debris; the tree was later replaced with a cedar tree. Even in the face of judgment, the United States, under the leadership of a burning Bush and corrupt men, planted—literally, by planting the cedar to replace the sycamore—their rebellion into the soil of New York.

On September 12, 2001, Senate Majority Leader Tom Daschle, in a speech to a joint session of Congress, proclaimed—or, better yet, attempted to prophesy—Isaiah 9:10. At the end of his speech he added prophetically, "This is what we will do. We will rebuild."[4] What was really being spoken would rise up to seize the soul of this nation twenty years later. "Oh yeah, we are going to *build back better.*" The seeds were planted right there in Congress for this slogan of rebellion that would rise up as a serpent decades later.

THE WEIMAR ALTAR

Looking back at our history, there were multiple defining moments that indeed led to what we see today. I call New York the carotid artery to Washington, DC. It feeds DC a lot of what it needs, and it has an insatiable appetite that feeds off corruption, defiance, and manipulation that affects an entire nation.

To understand the deceptive revelations, propaganda, and weaponization of "freedom" the enemy has utilized to destroy the moral and spiritual foundation of this nation, we must look at a paradigm that mirrors in many ways what is happening in our nation—and other nations as well. The enemy works in cycles; understanding the cycles exposes how he will mutate revelations of ancient demons and territorial spirits to cause generations to accept such deceptions, lies, and power that are impure in every sense. To understand these cycles, we must examine the mystery of the Weimar Republic in Germany.

The Weimar Republic was the German government that existed between the end of World War I in 1918 and the rise of Nazi Germany in 1933, before Hitler took power. A crucial movement occurred in Germany during that time. This movement was a major key that unlocked a door in the Weimar Republic that spiritually weakened and subdued it as prey for the taking and cleared the path for Hitler and the enemy's solutions to arise.

Resulting from World War I, the Weimar Republic saw a blatant push for the LGBTQ+ agenda and transgenderism. These agendas being pushed by the enemy's "agents of light" weakened the family unit and the country's morals and opened the door spiritually for the entire nation to become full-on oppressed. The police tolerated gay bars, which was one reason that Berlin became a global center for gay prostitution. Basically, the police were told to back off and tolerate. Sound familiar? There was also a growing gay civil rights movement in Berlin, led by Magnus Hirschfeld, a German Jewish physician and sexologist. For tyranny to enter through the gate of a nation, it must first be gravely spiritually compromised and its morals obliterated. It goes back to the garden: "Did God really say...?"

German Jews experienced a period of increased social and economic freedom during the Weimar Republic. Culturally, the period produced important and lasting results. As historian Peter Gay writes, "The Republic created little; it liberated what was already there."[5]

German prosperity in the late 1920s was problematic because, as it was the post-WWI environment, the nation was very much dependent on foreign credit. That should also sound familiar. When the sources of credit disappeared and loans were called in—yes, banks called in loans even though Germany was on a financial slippery slope—Germany faced an economic crisis more severe than any other country. It was a significant economic decline in every sense.[6] Because of the economic situation combined with the high cost of reparations, the German government faced a classic dilemma: cut government spending to try to balance the budget or increase it in an attempt to jump-start the economy. The German government just kept printing money without anything of substance backing it, which led to hyperinflation.

Germany was already facing economic disaster by the end of the 1920s, but it got worse.

October 14, 1929, was Yom Kippur, the holiest day on the Jewish calendar. It is the Day of Atonement, a day of reckoning. Ten days after Yom Kippur, on a day now known as Black Thursday, the US stock market crashed. The US had been experiencing a bull market, but on October 24, 1929, the bull crashed; America's golden calf, Baal, crashed. The Great Depression hit the world like a plague. And when plagues occur, desperation sets in.

The year 1929 was a *shemitah* on the Jewish calendar. The shemitah happens every seven years, and it is a year of release, requiring Jews to let farmland lie fallow for a year and to forgive all debts. Major world events are known to occur during shemitah years. (The next shemitah year will be in 2028, our next election year.)

In July 1931 one of Germany's largest financial institutions, Darmstadt and National Bank, collapsed. Two months later the unemployment figure reached 4.3 million.[7] Given that about 60 percent of the population typically makes up the workforce, this means over 11 percent of Germany's workforce was unemployed. This was seventy-seven years before the world financial and banking crisis of 2008—double sevens—and remember, every seven years is a shemitah.

Then, in the 1930s, in addition to all the other issues happening in Germany, protests against Jews and Jewish students broke out at universities across the country. Laws were also passed preventing Jews from holding official positions, including as professors. The result was that Jewish students and professors were driven out of the universities.

These elements all coming together paved the way for Hitler to come to power. The rise of homosexuality and transgenderism severely weakened the family unit and morality in general. It opened a portal, a liberal portal. The dependency on foreign credit, the intense rise of the national debt, the Great Depression, and protests against Jews all came together in a perfect storm and paved the way for a false visionary, a false prophet, to arise, one who would peddle and prop up the enemy's vision and attempt world domination ahead of schedule.

Hitler was an instrument from hell with the goal of total destruction of God's people, but the covenant of the Lord was with them, an everlasting covenant. The Lord also has a schedule, and the enemy does not get to jump ahead of it. Events are allowed to take place that ultimately push that timeline back in place. Second Thessalonians 2:3–6 (NASB) says:

> Let no one in any way deceive you, for it will not come unless the apostasy comes first, and the man of lawlessness is revealed, the son of destruction, who opposes and exalts himself above every so-called god or object of worship, so that he takes his seat in the temple of God, displaying himself as being God. Do you not remember that while I was still with you, I was telling you these things? And you know what restrains him now, so that in his time he will be revealed.

During all these difficult circumstances, there was a presidential election in Germany. President Hindenburg, who was eighty-four years old with failing health, decided to run for reelection in 1932, as he was the only candidate who could defeat Adolf Hitler, whom he saw as a dangerous extremist. Others shared his opinion of Hitler, including Dietrich Bonhoeffer, a prophet and visionary who sounded the alarm about the lukewarmness and absolute ignorance of the Protestant church amid these events.

There was a push for churches to be mouthpieces of Nazi propaganda, including anti-Semitism, as well as for theology and doctrine to be changed to fit the purposes and beliefs of the Nazis. There were about eighteen thousand Protestant pastors in Germany when Hitler rose to power. About three thousand of them stood with Bonhoeffer and others, known as the Confessing Church, who called for the church to resist such satanic tyranny. About the same number of pastors stood with Hitler, either bought and paid for or controlled by fear, and as spiritually blind as bats. But about two-thirds of pastors faltered between two opinions and spoke not a word.[8] They wanted to remain neutral. Silence in the face of evil is still evil.

A German pastor from that time who initially supported Hitler—but then realized the truth and ended up spending

seven years in a concentration camp for opposing Hitler—
famously said:

> First they came for the socialists, and I did not speak
> out—because I was not a socialist.
> Then they came for the trade unionists, and I did
> not speak out—because I was not a trade unionist.
> Then they came for the Jews, and I did not speak
> out—because I was not a Jew.
> Then they came for me—and there was no one left
> to speak for me.[9]

Had even a few thousand of the pastors who remained "neutral" stood with the Confessing Church instead, preaching
the truth of the Word of God even if it was unpopular or
not politically correct, Hitler may never have come to power.
The role of the church is crucial in protecting a nation from
ruthless and predatory evil deployed from the pits of hell.

But because all these factors were converging, Hindenburg,
who won the presidency, was pressured to make Hitler the
chancellor because of the popularity of the Nazi party and
how many votes it had received in the election. Hindenburg
appointed a sociopath to run the government and poised
Germany to be led in chains down a road of perdition and
destruction, with the spirits of lawlessness and murder as the
ringleaders of a diabolical takeover.

PERGAMON, SATAN'S THRONE

The ancient city of Pergamum, also known as Pergamon, was
a bustling city and Asia Minor's focal point of pagan worship.
It was destroyed and rebuilt several times, but it eventually
stood in ruins. Then, in the 1860s, Carl Humann, a German
engineer, began excavating it and eventually found the Altar

of Zeus, considered one of the greatest monuments of the ancient world. The altar was excavated and taken to Berlin, where it was reassembled in the Pergamon Museum.

The altar found in Pergamon has another name. The Book of Revelation contains letters to seven churches, including the church at Pergamum:

> And to the angel of the church in Pergamum write:
> The One who has the sharp two-edged sword says this:
> "I know where you dwell, where Satan's throne is; and you hold fast My name, and did not deny My faith even in the days of Antipas, My witness, My faithful one, who was killed among you, where Satan dwells."
> —REVELATION 2:12–13, NASB

The Pergamon Altar is also called Satan's throne. With the approval of the Turkish government, the altar became the official property of Germany. In 1930 the Pergamon Museum housing the altar was completed and opened to the public, sixty-six years after Humann first went to Pergamon and three years before Hitler was made chancellor of Germany.

> A few years later, the Nazi Party's chief architect, Albert Speer, was commissioned by the new chancellor, Adolf Hitler, to design the parade grounds for the party rallies in Nuremberg. Speer turned [or shall we say was turned by dark forces] to the Pergamon Altar for inspiration. Using the altar as a model, Speer created an enormous grandstand, known as the *Zeppelin tribune*. In the following years' mass rallies, Hitler descended down the steps like a tribune in ancient Rome.[10]

Most of the rallies in Nuremberg were held at night. They illuminated the darkness with many lights, creating an effect known as the Cathedral of Light. From the altar to the "cathedral" to the holy oath the Nazis swore, Hitler put on a show as a false prophet. Nuremberg was also the eventual site of the Nuremberg trials, where ten Nazi officers were hanged on October 16, 1946, just as the ten sons of Haman were hanged in the Book of Esther after the attempted annihilation of the Jewish people. History often repeats itself with the consequences of attacking a people in an active covenant with the Lord.

Six years after Hitler was made chancellor of Germany—six being the number of man—World War II began. The United States did what so many Protestant pastors in Germany did—look the other way and say, "We want to stay neutral and not get involved." I am not by any stretch of the imagination in favor of getting involved in foreign wars unnecessarily. However, what Hitler was doing was far beyond the scope of many wars; it was a plan to swallow up the nations and combine governments together into one world government—with Hitler at the top.

The sixty-six-year interval related to the Altar of Zeus and the Pergamon Museum, and the six years between Hitler becoming chancellor and the war beginning combine to 666, the number of the beast, of the man of sin described in the Book of Revelation. These are the cycles we must pay attention to.

PEARL HARBOR

The United States did not enter the war until more than two years after it started. America had been hesitant to engage Hitler, despite his barbaric extermination of the Jews and quest for world domination. It was an event that unfolded, a surprise attack, that opened a gate for the United States to join the fight. It was a pearl gate.

The weakening of our nation's foundation advanced on December 7, 1941, with the bombing of Pearl Harbor. Many warnings of this impending attack were ignored.

Why a port named Pearl Harbor? Well, let's examine how pearls are created. "Mollusks make pearls as a protection against irritants that sneak into their soft tissue. They do so by exuding layer upon layer of shell material. For some animals, this material is nacre, or mother of pearl."[11] It's like they are binding up an intruder to keep the intruder from causing damage.

Pearls are created because of intruders that do not belong, and measures are taken to insulate the threat. The military base at Pearl Harbor was there as protection against intruders, a way to protect the United States from threats.

Revelation 21:21 (NKJV) says, "The twelve gates were twelve pearls: each individual gate was of one pearl. And the street of the city was pure gold, like transparent glass." Just as the gates in the New Jerusalem were made of pearl, Pearl Harbor acted as a gate. When it was bombed, it opened a gate for the United States to enter the war. In that war the United States faced two men who foreshadowed the antichrist, the man of sin described in 2 Thessalonians 2:3. Both Hitler and Emperor Hirohito emerged on the world scene as Satan's trophies, charismatic visionaries who would be utilized to bulldoze freedom and godliness as their plans of regional and world domination unfolded.

Hitler's first name, Adolf, means wolf, and wolves hunt in packs. Hitler was born April 20, 1889, on the fifth day of Passover that year. Passover originated in the Book of Exodus. The Egyptian Pharaoh enslaved the Jews and had their babies killed. A boy named Moses escaped being killed and was raised in Pharaoh's own court. God then hid him in the wilderness for forty years and sent him back to Egypt to help rescue and free the Jewish people. Pharaoh refused to let them go, so the Lord sent ten plagues, the last of which was the death of the firstborn of every family in Egypt, including Pharaoh's. The only way to escape the plague was to spread the blood of a lamb on the doorpost of your house, which would cause the Lord to "pass over the door and not allow the destroyer to come into your houses to strike you" (Exod. 12:23, NKJV)—hence the name Passover.

It is no mistake that Hitler was born when he was; it was a marker, the enemy's own revelation of the war he would bring to Germany, Europe, and the world—a war against the covenant of God, a war against God's children, a war against God himself. That war even birthed the propaganda machine we see at work today. Germany was a common denominator in both world wars, and Germany is Gomer in Ezekiel 38, the war of Ezekiel, a war that is yet to come but once again will involve Germany.

Hirohito, on the other war front, was more than just Japan's head of state. He was considered its monarch by divine right and "the personification of both the nation and its spiritual imperative for imperial expansion."[12] Hitler and Hirohito were two titans who arose looking for imperial domination, bringing with it the chains of tyranny.

There are many similarities between Germany in the years leading up to World War II and the current state of the United States—the devaluing of life, anti-Semitism, economic crises, the pushing of the LGBTQ+ agenda, a massive propaganda machine, and a church that is largely asleep or lukewarm. The rebellion against the truth was leading to judgment. The German church needed to wake up or warm up, just as the American church needs to wake up or warm up today.

We can see the enemy's tactics at work as he pushes us further and further down the road to rebellion and judgment. We have an opportunity to make a change. We have an opportunity to speak the truth with boldness and call the nation to repentance. We have an opportunity to reverse our direction as a nation, turning us back to the Creator, to almighty God, and bringing revival.

AFTER THE WAR

World War II led to what is known as the Cold War, the war against the rise of communism. Communism was birthed out of satanism.

Karl Marx, who wrote *The Communist Manifesto*, also wrote plays that contained satanic undertones and beliefs. This is taken from a poem he wrote:

> How so! I plunge, plunge without fail
> My blood-black sabre into your soul.
> That art God neither wants nor wists,
> It leaps to the brain from Hell's black mists.
>
> Till heart's bewitched, till senses reel:
> With Satan I have struck my deal.
> He chalks the signs, beats time for me,
> I play the death march fast and free.[13]

In letters Marx's son even called him "my dear devil."[14] This was the foundation Satan laid through his slaves and servants who were the building blocks of tyranny and of what we see happening in the world today.

The serpent is the commander, author, and peddler of

communism, tyranny, imperialism, and, of course, satanism. What Satan could not accomplish in a rebellion against God in heaven he has obsessively fought to accomplish on earth.

Satan has used many weapons in the spiritual war being waged on earth. He has used tyranny, deception, and lies, among other things, but he has also used music. This went into overdrive in the early 1950s with the emergence of rock and roll. The name alone could be considered a mockery of Christ's resurrection, when a rock was rolled away from the tomb. Satan's trophies and prophetic voices were sent out in a small army to allure the young of the nation using a tool he knew oh so very well: music.

Music opens the soul, so the enemy uses it to open the soul of a nation. The enemy's messages are sent out across the airwaves of the nation. One of the key groups was The Beatles, with songs such as "Lucy in the Sky with Diamonds" (which many interpret as being about LSD), "Revolution," and "Lady Madonna" that in many ways were spells falling upon the nation and ensnaring the souls of men. Their name is interesting, as beetles can be highly invasive and eat up the good crop. Another group was The Rolling Stones (whose name can also be considered a mockery of Christ's resurrection), which released songs such as "Beast of Burden," "Sympathy for the Devil," and "Paint It Black."

Both these groups came over to the United States from England, the country whose hand of tyranny ruled over the colonies of the yet-to-be-formed United States. The Revolutionary War was fought to break free of this tyranny. The Constitution and Declaration of Independence were birthed from this historic victory over England. The enemy, who comes as an angel of light to deceive humanity, in his cunningness found a new way to utilize the spirit that operated through England and its tyranny, a new way to come and put America back in chains. This new strategy used these groups who sold their souls to the devil for power and fame. The enemy *never* forgot the defeat of the American Revolution, so he concocted a new kind of invasion. Remember, these rock groups coming to the United States was called the British invasion.

When the era of rock and roll was ushered into the nation, drugs and free love followed. Free love was the opposite of real love, and it flew in the face of Jesus' sacrifice, the price Christ paid for the sins of humanity on the cross. Drugs and music opened souls wide and put a welcome mat out for every foul and unclean spirit to come and set up shop rent-free. Lucifer took with him when he fell the gift God had given him for music when he was created. He raised up a dark empire from it. You could say the empire definitely struck back. Satan utilized the freedom of the nation to introduce these spiritual nuclear bombs that would ravage the nation's sense of godliness and morality. So many in our nation failed to understand that freedom is liberty with responsibility, not an excuse to live as if you are at one long and reckless frat party.

The events that occurred in the 1950s tilled the soil for what was about to hit the nation. The nation was enticed through drugs, rock and roll, and the romanticizing of rebellion. At that point, the soul of the nation and the souls of men were opened up, and many messages were spoken prophetically through the music airwaves. This caused the nation to become ripe for a forsaking, a turning away from God. "One nation under God" was about to face a decades-long onslaught to dismantle the covenant between God and the United States. It was a calculated attack, intended to strike at the very core of what the United States was meant to be and inherently change the fabric of the nation.

As we look at some of the events that were part of the nation's rebellion against God, it is interesting how they often connect to other strategies and tactics of the kingdom of darkness, both here in the United States and around the world. Friedrich Engels was a German philosopher and revolutionary socialist. As we know, socialism leads to Communism, and Engels was Karl Marx's closest collaborator. They authored *The Communist Manifesto* together.

Communism and atheism go hand in hand. The enemy will utilize similar tactics to perpetuate the spiritual cycle of rebellion that moves his agenda forward. If we compare Engels' last name to an important event that happened in the United States, we see a connection.

A crucial cornerstone was removed from this nation's foundation during the 1960s when *Engel v. Vitale* came before the Supreme Court and became the source of a public battle. The New York State Board of Regents' prayer that caused the lawsuit was:

> Almighty God, we acknowledge our dependence upon
> Thee, and we beg Thy blessings upon us, our parents,
> our teachers and our Country.[15]

The Supreme Court ruling caused prayer to be removed from schools across the nation. Engels was a collaborator of Communism; Engel was a member of a humanist society that believed "morality is independent of theology,"[16] and he was one of the driving forces behind the lawsuit. Do you see the connection?

The *Engel v. Vitale* decision caused a national uproar. Judges are supposed to be representations of almighty God on this earth, as He is the righteous judge. Judges are supposed to rule through a lens of righteousness. The Supreme

Court's enormous failure to do so in just this one instance has had a severe ripple effect that continues to the present day. All the prayer, praise, and agreement was stripped from the education system of this nation, leaving a gaping hole that the enemy went right through.

The serpent strategically made arguments through atheists that opened the door to far worse in the following decades. The education system became an empty temple of sorts. By evicting the Lord from education of the younger generation, deceived and ignorant men and women opened a portal for the enemy to come in with every agenda from hell to attempt to destroy children. Deception and lies began to enter the portal, and they haven't stopped. The strategy was to change the way children are taught and mold them into minions rather than critical thinkers who understand that almighty God exists and needs to be part of their lives.

This was the first planting of invasive tares that would grow with the wheat and choke out the good crop (Matt. 13:24–30). The invasion continued. We now see this generation covered with invasive weeds, tares, deception, and lies that choke their purpose and chain their minds to everything dark. The enemy is destroying their discernment so that when he appears as an angel of light, they will continue to be deceived, evil will appear good, and good will appear evil. What happened with *Engel v. Vitale* was meant to tear apart the fabric of this nation and make "one nation under God, indivisible" now be easily divisible.

The removal of prayer from schools was just one strategy of a multipart attack. To change a nation foundationally, the enemy must change who they pray to, change who they serve, divide them, and redirect the sacrificial offerings to benefit the kingdom of darkness. When these things happen, combined with false prophets and showmen, rebellion, lukewarmness, mass deception, and other tactics of the enemy, it puts the nation on a collision course.

Once these voices of deception were able to turn the highest court in the land, it opened a locked gate—one that ancient Israel opened themselves and paid a very severe price for. About ten years later, in the 1970s, abortion was legalized. Just as the plan was hatched in New York to take prayer out of schools, so the plan was hatched in New York to bring abortion to the national stage and fiercely push to legalize it. Remember, if the enemy changes the way a generation prays—or prevents them from praying—it is far easier to sway them to sacrifice for the enemy's interests.

Roe v. Wade opened the floodgates of destruction in this nation, with Margaret Sanger, Ruth Bader Ginsberg, and other prophets of Ashtoreth paving a path of blood for the nation in the very direction George Washington, under inspiration of the Lord, had warned against. The nation had turned away from God, so the blessings of God would be removed. This was a road to perdition being paved in the name of tolerance and choice. "My body, my choice" is a narcissistic, hypocritical, self-serving slogan when another body is involved, the body of an innocent child. Second Timothy 3:1–5 (NASB) says:

> But realize this, that in the last days difficult times will come. For men will be lovers of self, lovers of money, boastful, arrogant, revilers, disobedient to parents, ungrateful, unholy, unloving, irreconcilable, malicious gossips, without self-control, brutal, haters of good, treacherous, reckless, conceited, lovers of pleasure rather than lovers of God, holding to a form of godliness, although they have denied its power; avoid such men as these.

Isn't it fascinating how "my body, my choice" applies when someone wants to kill a baby, but it suddenly no longer applied and was even demonized when it came to getting an untested COVID-19 vaccination? Suddenly the very groups who concocted such an ideology were quick to say "my body, my choice" does not apply to dangerous potions being injected into people's bodies.

Oswald Chambers said, "Sin is more than moral irregularity. It is a disposition to follow one's own way rather than God's way."[17] This is exactly what took hold of the nation. It was all part of the cycle, all part of the enemy's plan to push the nation further down the road of rebellion. A group of corrupt men and women with broken dispositions and souls and deranged minds said, "We have a better way where you can do what thou wilt." You can do whatever you want, and that's the law; identify as whatever you want, say whatever you want. That is a recipe for chaos because there is no standard. They encouraged the masses to deny reality and accept *their* narrative, their "truth," because it's a *better* way, a way that is *tolerant* and will keep you *safe*—all the buzz words needed to make people fall for the deception.

Corrupt men know nothing about safety of the mind, soul, and spirit because they were lured by "Did God really say…?" and now use it to lure others into their rebellion. It is the same playbook from the Garden of Eden, reworked for a modern generation: Create doubt in the minds of humanity; committing to an alternative way that strays toward dangerous ditches will soon follow. These wicked men and women behind the most toxic and destructive of agendas know the soul and the body are connected. The master puppeteer who is controlling them, the enemy, knows this well. Feed the flesh, overindulge the flesh, and every desire that is at enmity with God, the mind, and the soul will become a tool for the enemy's agendas.

His soothsayers and false prophets are out in an army across the airwaves, protesting in the streets, and deceiving boards of education and universities across the land. Man, under the deception of the serpent, has set himself up as the alpha, the all-knowing being in the highest seat of judgment and authority. It is a continuation of the spiritual cycle, pushing the public more and more to rebellion against authority and rejection of God. The showmen and false prophets are deceiving people into using their free will given by God to go around God, to build their own Babel, their own morality, and their own worship. But that is a foundation built on sand.

If a nation builds a dysfunctional, toxic, immoral, and deceptive platform on sand, when the storm comes and the wind blows and the waves crash, the foundation will be washed away and everything built on it will come crashing down. It's like building a sandcastle; it won't hold up against water. The puppets of the enemy have built a sandcastle, thinking it will stand against the water of the Word of God. But there is a time and season for everything under heaven (Eccles. 3:1), and their intricate sandcastles face a tidal wave that is rising—the truth, the Word of God, spoken and prophesied and declared and obeyed by believers willing to take a stand against the kingdom of darkness, believers who are ready for a return to a godly moral standard in this nation. "So shall they fear the name of the LORD from the west, and His glory from the rising of the sun; when the enemy comes in like a flood, the Spirit of the LORD will lift up a standard against him" (Isa. 59:19, NKJV).

CHAPTER 10

A NATIONAL IDENTITY CRISIS

MANY IN THE church were lulled right into being part of a detailed plan to bring them down to lukewarm and utilize the church as a weapon to promote the enemy's agendas. When did such allurement happen? We must go back to 2008 to understand when the nation took a dangerous turn.

The year 2008 was a shemitah. Remember, a shemitah occurs every seven years. After seven shemitah cycles (forty-nine years), the next year, the fiftieth year, is the Jubilee, a year of release and return. Events of serious national importance having to do with finances, land, security, and so forth happen quite often during a shemitah year.

THEY ASKED FOR IT

In 2008 a candidate emerged as a presidential hopeful. He was a Saul. The name Saul means "asked for." When the children of Israel asked for a king so they could be like other nations, the Lord told the prophet Samuel, "Listen to the voice of the people in regard to all that they say to you, for they have not rejected you, but they have rejected Me from being king over them" (1 Sam. 8:7, NASB). Then the Lord gave them Saul, the one they asked for, to be king over them.

The children of Israel rejected God as their leader, and the United States followed suit in what they did as a nation. Just as the people of Israel wanted a king and a way that was not the Lord's, so did the United States. They asked for it, and in 2008 it happened. His name was Barack Obama.

In Hebrew, Barak means several things, including lightning. Who is associated with lightning? Satan, who comes as an angel of light. In Luke 10:18, Jesus said, "I was watching Satan fall from heaven like lightning" (NASB). Obama means to lean or bend. This was the entirety of Obama's campaign and presidency summed up—come in as a light for the one who fell as lightning and cause the nation and the masses to lean and bend in the direction of the enemy's agenda. This charismatic candidate and his party lured the people into drifting further from the Lord and His ways. Satan is the father of lies, and his trophies have no issue with smiling genuinely while lying fully. Obama's campaign slogan was "Yes, we can," kind of like his running mate's future slogan, "Build back better"—each has three words.

During 2008, a shemitah year and an election year, Obama emerged fully on the scene. It was also the year a severe banking crisis hit America and the world. The global financial crisis of the time was the most significant and damaging economic crisis since the Great Depression started in 1929. This was a serious warning to America of what was to come.

Seven years earlier, in 2001 (also a shemitah year), after the Twin Towers went down, the cry of defiance and rebellion was Isaiah 9:10: "The bricks have fallen down, but *we will rebuild* with hewn stones" (NKJV, emphasis added). In 2008 we began to see the result of the sheer defiance by American leadership. It opened a gate for a candidate such as Obama to emerge with his charismatic deception. In Obama's victory speech he said, "But tonight, because of what we did on this day, in this election, at this defining moment, *change has come to America.*...The road ahead will be long. Our climb will be steep. We may not get there in one year, or even one term, but America—I have never been more hopeful than I am tonight that we will get there."[1]

Obama intentionally did not make it clear what kind of change had come to America; it was portrayed as an incredible change, a hopeful change, as the enemy always veils his true intentions with what appears to be help and hope. But a change had come, all right—one that accelerated America on a road to perdition and rebellion against God's order.

God's sacred order of time is for everything to go from darkness to light. Genesis 1:5 says, "And there was evening and there was morning, one day." Evening and then morning—for darkness has to submit and give way to the light. In 2008 the enemy tried to interfere with that sacred order of time and have darkness overtake the light. It is a grave violation of God's law and order for Satan and men to tamper with that order, but they did. Obama, as a prophetic voice of darkness and deceit, lulled the people into thinking he would provide them everything they wanted. That fact, as well as the fact that he was the first black president, overshadowed the pronounced discrepancies in his character, beliefs, and red herring of a plan. Those that entertain the spirit of antichrist at their tables tend to follow in some way the path that the true antichrist, the man of sin, will take. Charles Spurgeon once said, "Man's mouth, though it be but a little hole, will hold a world full of sin. For there is not any sin forbidden in the law or gospel which is not spoken by the tongue."[2]

We suddenly saw high-profile pastors—who were supposed to be looking out for the interests of this nation, speaking and preaching the truth, and upholding the biblical standard that had been chiseled away at for decades—forsake the Word of God because of the color of Obama's skin. Skin color became the idol of the 2008 presidential election.

Martin Luther King Jr. famously and poignantly said, "I have a dream that my four little children will one day live in a nation where they will not be judged by the color of their skin but by the content of their character."[3] Content of character bowed to skin pigmentation as the idea of the nation's first black president was romanticized, whether or not he was qualified, and whether or not he would lead the nation in the right direction. Skin color eclipsed Obama's veiled past, with far too many discrepancies and issues that were overlooked.

Let me be clear: It will be the gross overlooking of such issues on a world stage that will pave the way for the antichrist, the man of sin, to come to power. This was a dress rehearsal of sorts, a test of our biblical alert system. And here were high-profile pastors, as well as pastors of small local churches, who ignored the biblical alert system of the Holy Spirit and helped many in the church to idolize skin color. The enemy had a tempting piece of fruit, but the church should have known to stay away. Too many pastors and shepherds led their flocks to ignore every red flag and violation of biblical standards in order to make history for the black community.

The year 2008 was the year 5768 to 5769 on the Jewish calendar. The year 5769 was the first year of a new seven-year shemitah cycle. The numbers in 5769 translate into a sentence that prophetically spoke about Obama's presidency: "Yes indeed, this world has forgotten about God, and I have a feeling He is about to remind us who He is."

During Obama's first term, the Great Recession gripped the nation. It was reminiscent of the Weimar Republic, the stock market crash of 1929, and the ushering in of the Great Depression. There was a series of triggering events, including irresponsible deals executed by banks, that "began with the bursting of the United States housing bubble in 2005–2012. When housing prices fell and homeowners began to abandon their mortgages, the value of mortgage-backed securities held by investment banks went down in 2007–2008. This caused many banks to collapse or be bailed out in September 2008."[4] The campaign slogan may have been "Yes, we can," but the financial crisis took hold, causing the sustained recession that plagued Obama's first term.

Obama's first term, with a dark cloud of recession looming over it, was basically a campaign of what a great guy and leader he was, giving the *illusion* that he was solving the issues within the United States and even other parts of the world. The illusion lured people in so that in his second term the darkest part of this agenda would be able to unfold. This would occur by the hand and pen not just of Obama but also of those around him, including Valerie Jarrett and Hillary Clinton. His court with the prophets of Baal and Ashtoreth set the agendas.

The enemy was using the same tactics he always does, using deception and lies to lead humanity astray, and as a nation our loss of identity as "one nation under God" was accelerating rapidly.

On June 14, 2012, Obama signed a beam at One World Trade Center: "We remember. We rebuild. We come back stronger."[5] Oh yeah, we are going to build back better. The bricks have fallen, but we will rebuild. Do you see how those same words of rebellion have been repeated time and time again?

On December 14, 2012, the Sandy Hook shooting occurred. Prophetically I want to point out that the name Sandy Hook is what the nation was in after Obama won reelection. The United States was hooked in sand—quicksand.

Proverbs 27:3 (NASB) says, "A stone is heavy and the sand weighty, but the provocation of a fool is heavier than both of them." On Obama's watch the national identity crisis turned our foundation to sand:

> Therefore everyone who hears these words of Mine and acts on them, may be compared to a wise man who built his house on the rock. And the rain fell, and the floods came, and the winds blew and slammed against that house; and yet it did not fall, for it had been founded on the rock. Everyone who hears these words of Mine and does not act on them, will be like a foolish man who built his house on the sand. The rain fell, and the floods came, and the winds blew and slammed against that house; and it fell—and great was its fall.
>
> —MATTHEW 7:24–27, NASB

"And great was its fall."

OBAMA'S SECOND TERM

When initially asked to define *marriage*, Obama said it "is the union between a man and a woman."[6] Remember this for a moment. As far as abortion, Planned Parenthood Action Fund told its members on November 9, 2009, that "President Obama campaigned on a promise to put reproductive health care at the center of his reform plan."[7] Marriage and life came into serious play during Obama's second term.

In March of 2012, an election year, Obamacare was signed into law, offering the nation health insurance for those who could not afford it. Obama appeared as a champion. However, a stipulation in the Affordable Care Act requiring vaccines to be covered—and paving the way for vaccines to be pushed on people—was a medical and mortar path being carved for what would hit the nation and the world in 2020. Obama was packaged as a savior, a champion of the people, and charismatic, but the package really contained a cunning snake.

Genesis 3:1 says, "Now the serpent was more crafty (subtle, skilled in deceit) than any living creature of the field which the Lord God had made." Obama's "Yes, we can" was the defiant answer to God's standards that say, "No, you can't"—and not because God wants to limit our freedom but because He loves us enough to not want us to do things that are harmful.

In 2012 Mitt Romney was the Republican nominee who ran against Obama. Romney *appeared*—key word—to have the right heart posture, qualifications, and experience to be president. He was a Mormon. So you had a Mormon running against a closet Muslim—yes, I think Obama is a closet Muslim. Two faiths, both of which are missing a cornerstone, were contending in the race.

Obama's campaign slogan was "Forward." He wanted to continue to move forward in rebellion and till the soil for the plot of 2016, to move forward in defiance of the covenant and foundation of this nation. On November 6, 2012, Election Day, the fabric and morals of the nation inherently changed. The group emerging in America had global ties and was put in place to transform the soul of the nation, strip it of godliness and morality, and send it headlong into lawlessness, recklessness, and chaos—causing an identity crisis like the nation had never experienced. The enemy thrives in disorder; this was no different.

Obama once again won that election; the Lord allowed it. These were Saul years for the nation. The nation thought it was what they wanted. However, it would soon turn to madness, just like Saul's kingship in 1 Samuel. Saul was a charismatic man who turned against the ways of God for a rebellious agenda. Samuel, a true prophet of the Lord, said

to Saul in 1 Samuel 15:23 (NKJV), "For rebellion is as the sin
of witchcraft, and stubbornness is as iniquity and idolatry.
Because you have rejected the word of the LORD, He also has
rejected you from being king."

Obama's second term happened because the nation and a
good percentage of the church were hanging out in a wading
pool of lukewarmness and the zip code of "I do not want to
be involved." The root of liberalness was taking full effect—
liberal, "do what thou wilt shall be the whole of the Law."[8]
Liberalness is another word for *rebellion*. People were allowing
Obama to lure them right in. The Lord allowed it because
the church failed to raise a standard and instead entertained
the delicate dainties of deceit that marked Obama's terms.
Faltering between two opinions will lead to a valley of crisis.
The church faltered, and many "did not want to get involved,"
which gave the enemy an open door.

Mysteriously—or not so mysteriously—events began to
unfold in the second term like dominoes falling one after
the other.

There was a huge push for gun control, Lois Lerner admitted
that conservative groups seeking tax-exempt status were targeted by the IRS, the Edward Snowden documents exposed
the NSA's surveillance programs, a deeper racial divide than
ever before fractured the nation… Rebellion, stepping away
from the nation's Judeo-Christian values and onto a road of
perdition, led to these nation-altering events. When a Saul is
leading a nation, rebellion follows.

In 2014 another gate was opened because the enemy per-
ceived the weak leadership at the helm of the United States.
ISIS happened. The group is horrifically demonic, but Obama
played down the threat because some of the same ideologies
were indeed in the White House. These were all prophetic
puzzle pieces.

Something very prophetic happened in the nation on June 6, 2015. It is not spoken of often, but it was a big red arrow of warning about the turn this nation was about to take. That day, a horse named American Pharaoh won the Triple Crown in horse racing. Winning the Triple Crown is a difficult feat (it hadn't been won since 1978), and I took notice of the name immediately. It was a serious warning to the nation of where Obama wanted to take the United States.

Pharaohs were considered gods themselves, they worshipped false gods, they led their nations into the sin of idol worship, and they wore serpents on their heads. In fact, there is a false god of Egypt called Apep, a giant serpent that embodies darkness and disorder. During the eclipse of April 2024, NASA fired three rockets named APEP. Darkness and disorder were exactly what the nation was about to dive headlong into with the Obama presidency. He was going for the triple crown: three races, three terms, the first two already won by Obama, and the third he would try to win by using an extension of himself.

Then came June 26, 2015. June has become known as Pride Month. Proverbs 16:18 (kjv) says, "Pride goeth before destruction, and an haughty spirit before a fall." Pride is blinding, it blocks out warnings of danger, and it deceives people into doubling down on what will ultimately destroy them. It works the same with people and with nations.

In what I call the Sodom ruling, the Supreme Court handed down its decision in *Obergefell v. Hodges* on June 26, 2015. Isn't it interesting that the word *fell* is in that name? By a margin of one vote, the court ruled that same-sex marriage cannot be banned in the United States and that same-sex marriages must be recognized nationwide, granting same-sex couples the same rights as heterosexual couples under the law.

They called it a milestone for civil rights, but it was more like a millstone being hung around the neck of America. It would lead to far darker offshoots in the coming years. If America was in a recession, this was not going to rectify it. It was leading America into further disorder, far, far away from God's holy order. "The earth is the LORD's, and the fulness thereof" (Ps. 24:1, KJV).

Obama, the same man who said marriage was between one man and one woman, gave a "victory" speech—it was a victory for the enemy, but it truly was a defeat for the nation:

> This decision will end the patchwork system we currently have. It will end the uncertainty hundreds of thousands of same-sex couples face from not knowing whether their marriage, legitimate in the eyes of one state, will remain if they decide to move or even visit another. This ruling will strengthen all of our communities by offering to all loving same-sex couples the dignity of marriage across this great land.[9]

The Lord designed marriage to be between a man and a woman, but Obama offered up same-sex marriage like a buffet that the nation would feast on for years, making the nation sicker and sicker. The charismatic man that appeared to be a champion was truly a jailer, putting the nation in a cell of deception, rebellion, and sin. The match was lit, and a dumpster fire began. It was just one step in the plan to wage a war of perversion, especially on the young. It was a war of transhumanism, of transgenderism, of pronouns, intended to steal the identity of the upcoming generation until they were empty vessels that could be filled to the brim by demonic agendas. The enemy began a reprogramming process through broken vessels willing to do such heinous acts. This was a seed that grew into a man-eating weed.

The Supreme Court decision came near the beginning of

the 2016 campaign for president. The idea of "do whatever you want, and that's the law" echoed across the United States. The enemy hates freedom, especially through Christ. He hates moral order. He hates order within genders. He hates those who can think critically and measure what is being said on the news and in the lukewarm and apostate church against the Word of God. The evidence of all those things was clear in 2016.

CHAPTER 11

THE BATTLE FOR THE SOUL OF THE NATION

TEN DAYS BEFORE the Supreme Court ruling in *Oberge-fell v. Hodges*, on June 16, 2015, an outsider arose in the political arena, an outsider that had once been among them but had come out from among them. Real estate tycoon Donald J. Trump made the announcement that he was running for president.

Many laughed, made fun, and thought it was absolutely ridiculous; however, I could clearly see the Lord was about to hoodwink a lot of people. There is a biblical precedent that the Lord always raised up outsiders to lead Israel, including shepherds, orphans, and fishermen. Even tax collectors, who were definitely frowned upon by society, were called by Jesus Himself to be His disciples.

The prideful laugh at and mock many outsiders; how-ever, the Lord is putting a hook in their jaw and leading His enemies to their demise. Goliath laughed when David came before him to battle. He said, "Am I a dog, that you come to me with sticks?...Come to me, and I will give your flesh to the birds of the sky and the beasts of the field." But David said, "You come to me with a sword, a spear, and a javelin, but I come to you in the name of the LORD of hosts, the

God of the armies of Israel, whom you have taunted" (1 Sam. 17:43–45, NASB). David's declaration that he was coming in the name of the Lord is found in verse 45. The 2016 campaign was the race to be the forty-fifth president of the United States, and it was also someone taking on a giant. Many believers also connected Donald Trump's run to Isaiah 45, saying that Trump was a Cyrus.

MAKE AMERICA GODLY AGAIN

Approximately eight years earlier Kim Clement prophesied:

> There will be a praying president, not a religious one. For I will fool the people, says the Lord. I will fool the people, yes, I will. God says, the one that is chosen shall go in and they shall say, "He has hot blood." For the Spirit of God says, Yes, he may have hot blood, but he will bring the walls of protection on this country in a greater way and the economy of this country shall change rapidly, says the Lord of Hosts. Listen to the word of the Lord. God says, I will put at your helm for two terms a president that will pray, but he will not be a praying president when he starts. I will put him in office and then I will baptize him with the Holy Spirit and My power, says the Lord of Hosts....Trump shall become a trumpet, says the Lord....I will raise up the Trump to become a trumpet.[1]

He prophesied that Trump would become a trumpet, that he would be put in the office of president for two terms. Nothing was prophesied about two consecutive terms, just two terms.

After Trump announced his candidacy, a media typhoon unlike anything we had ever seen was forming. President Obama was positioned to go for the triple crown, for a third term through an extension of his inner circle, and Hillary Rodham Clinton announced she would run. President Obama wanted to be the American Pharaoh; he had an Egypt mentality. Let's examine Hillary's maiden name, Rodham, for a moment.

Rodham can be split into two words, *rod* and *Ham*. *Rod* can be defined as "a stick or bundle of twigs used to punish; a shepherd's cudgel; a pole with a line and usually a reel attached for fishing."[2] Ham was Noah's rebellious son who tried to humiliate him and was the father of Canaan, whom the idolatrous, pagan Canaanites descended from—the same Canaanites God ordained must be driven from the Promised Land. So Ham was associated with rebellion and idolatry. When we put it all together, Rodham means punisher, rebellion, shepherd of rebellion and idolatry, to reel in rebellion and idolatry.

That is no accident.

I remember having an open vision as this all unfolded. There was a tree, and it looked like a dead tree—not a leaf on it. Perching toward the bottom of the tree was a bald eagle. Suddenly a group of black crows closed in and began to torment the eagle. When this happened, the eagle shot up at a ninety-degree angle and perched atop the highest branch.

Donald Trump revealed the slogan "Make America great again," or MAGA. Hillary revealed the slogan "Stronger together"—even the enemy knows there is power in agreement. "Stronger together" was a Tower of Babel–like slogan for what they were proposing.

In order to make America great again, we must first make America godly again. There was this oxlike characteristic in Donald Trump—strong, powerful, and a bit reckless. Oxen must be yoked and steered by God.

When Trump was campaigning, he did not say what the

media, the government think tanks, the activist groups, and all the others who had been trying to control the narrative wanted him to say. He didn't act how they wanted. He didn't play by their rules. And boy, did he get an education in how dirty politics truly is, as those who once befriended him now turned on him and against him. He represented the ox that would be steered in the way to foil the Obama/Clinton triple crown.

Prophets were coming forth and validating what Kim Clement had seen so many years earlier, including a prophecy about one raised up out of New York to lead a nation gone astray. It had to be one raised out of New York because of that covenant George Washington made between the nation and God from New York City. To now attempt to save such a covenant, one had to be raised up out of New York who was brazen, a bit reckless, and not controllable by the beast of Washington, DC.

The person the Lord chooses many times is not who we, in our flesh, would choose for leadership. With presidential elections, we as the church have to understand that we are not voting for a pastor; we are voting for a leader. A leader can have qualities of a shepherd; however, they are inherently different. The prophet Samuel thought every one of David's brothers, one after the other, was the one God had chosen as the next king of Israel based on his appearance. David did not fit the bill of a king outwardly. But the Lord had searched the deepest places of his heart and found him worthy in a way that man could not see.

June 16, 2015, was the date of the escalator ride seen around the world. Donald Trump descended down that escalator. In order to ascend, we must first descend.

I remember that "prophets," especially in the African American community, arose prophesying a victory for Hillary. I thought, "Here is the company of Ahab's prophets saying, 'Go up to Ramoth Gilead, for the Lord will surely give you the victory.'" Gilead is where leaders are set up to fall; remember this.

The colosseum of media and technology with its false prophets went into overdrive, attacking Trump unlike anything we had ever seen. It was fake news—the enemy repeating lies over and over until the public perceives them as true. They would mix in a little bit of truth here and there to make their whole lot of lie look better. It goes back to that false company of prophets around Ahab who would all repeat each other, like mockingbirds, and prophesy falsely to attempt to sway outcomes.

It was the rod of Ham against the Trump—a trumpet that was loud and noisy and would name-call back and tweet like there was no tomorrow. Trump can also mean drum, so if the shoe fits...

In fact, if you look into the meaning of Donald Trump's full name, you see a profound prophetic statement emerge. Trump can mean drum, the sound of a trumpet used to announce, or the suit in card games that outranks all the other suits. Donald means ruler of the world, and his middle name, John, means God is gracious. If you put it all together, it means the ruler of the world will announce that God is gracious, and He will outrank all others.

THE CHAOS CANDIDATE

The liberal media and the Left were having a meltdown while mocking Trump's entrance into the race. The primaries were messy, to say the least. Trump was like a bull in a china shop, but he was on a path carved by the Lord, and he won the Republican nomination. All of Trump's brazenness, boldness, and sometimes inappropriateness was turning the political arena upside down. If we think about David, Joseph, and Cyrus, they all had a brazenness, ruggedness, and boldness that the Lord fashioned to help them lead during national crises. And in 2016 there were multiple crises cresting over the horizon like a tidal wave.

Prophetically speaking, the running mates chosen by the candidates had just as much prophetic significance as the main players themselves.

The vice presidential pick for Donald Trump was Ohio governor Mike Pence. Pence derives from Penn, which means enclosure or hill. On Hillary Clinton's side was Tim Kaine. Kaine equals Cain, which means acquired, as in bought and paid for. In the Bible, Cain betrayed his brother Abel because he was favored by God and brought a more acceptable sacrifice.

The rod of Ham and Cain was up against a drum or trumpet on a hill. The establishment was terrified of an outsider. The swamp creatures that lurked within Washington, DC, were frantic about Donald Trump winning because they could not control him. He used his *own money*; he sowed it into the soil of this nation, and it will not return void now.

Many pastors started to become vocal in their support of the chaos candidate they believed was commissioned to unravel the plans of wicked people and organizations that attempted to continue their well-orchestrated quest for power. There were images of large groups of pastors laying hands on and praying over this very unconventional candidate. This was also when the prophetic began to be moved into position for the catastrophic events that were on the horizon.

November 8, 2016, was a historic day in the history of America; it was the day the American Pharaoh was denied his triple crown. The media, the false prophets, and the mockingbirds were in utter shock at what was unfolding, as the liberal beast thought they had the election. It all fell like a house of cards. Their plans that they had laughed about and pridefully boasted about, and their mocking of the outsider, all failed. The same thing happened again in the 2024 election. The plans of the enemy failed because they were not battling an outsider— they were warring against the Lord and His plans and purposes, which are far beyond what humanity can comprehend and understand. What prophet Kim Clement, other prophets, and I had prophesied came to pass before our very eyes.

RESET

Three years into Donald Trump's first presidential term, the United States and the world were about to face an evil—an evil that was revelationary in nature, an evil that foreshadowed some events in the Book of Revelation.

On November 13, 2019, I received a word from the Lord. I had been publicly broadcasting for a year and a half, a good portion of that while my husband, Chris, was in the hospital after miraculously surviving a rupture of an arteriovenous malformation (AVM) in his brain and a hemorrhagic stroke. My life was seriously altered as I faced bringing home and caring for my husband, who was now disabled. I was prophesying from the Lord through this life-altering event. After a total of nine months in the hospital that year, my husband had been home only a week on that November day.

I delivered a word from the Lord, but I did not understand what was being spoken until it happened two months later. I was hearing the word *reset*. The Lord was doing a very large *reset* of people's lives. The Lord was resetting things back into position and in some cases freeing people in order to save them.

The reset involved countries as well, China being one of them. China is going to be dealt very heavy blows for the wickedness going on. Their whole train of contact with the elites is about to get derailed and run right off the tracks. The leader of China will be involved for what they have done to their people, and those who are sold out to this leader of industry will fall as well. The Chinese government wants to try to force believers to renounce the Lord. Well, the gavel has dropped, and the Lord has judged China and its leaders, and we shall see this come to pass. There is tension in China because there is tension in the realm of the spirit. A heavy blow is knocking on their door.

On December 8, 2019, I delivered a word from the Lord:

> There will be an awakening, a revival that breaks out in 2020, concentrated areas where My glory shall rest, and those who are weary and heavy laden will flock to those areas for the soothing balm of My spirit that shall act as a sanitizing agent and a healing balm, and deliverance shall break forth, says the Lord.

On December 12, 2019, I delivered another word from the Lord:

> I, the Lord God, am taking the axe to the diseased stumps of these branded and entangled messes, of these very crooked trees that grew in a winding and serpentlike fashion because their roots were drinking from the rivers of darkness, not of the living water of *My* Word, says the Lord. The sickle is the hook I, the Lord, speak of in Ezekiel, putting a hook in their jaw, and I, the Lord, am doing the same. I have put the hook in the core of what drives them—power, control, a thirst to oppress and depress in order to attempt to elevate their father the devil. I, the Lord, have put a hook in their jaw and in their core and am leading

them in their delusions and illusions while the axe is being taken to their stump. And soon *timber* shall be felled, and the crash will be loud, says the Lord, and send shock waves and fear amongst those who were doing their bidding who will now be caught.

These prophecies were being given because of what was about to happen. The shift and reset were happening in 2020!

It was a reset like we have never seen. For something to reset, it must first be allowed to break or shut down. At the beginning of January 2020, it all derailed. COVID-19 entered the world from a lab in Wuhan, China, and was released like a plague upon the earth.[3] Donald Trump was beginning a campaign for reelection when this happened. Events unfolded that we have not seen since the Great Depression. The enemy's agents went to work to deceive the president, the nation, and the world with their false revelations—deceptions that had layer upon layer of talking points and false data.

Ground zero for COVID-19 in the United States was New York City, the same place where fifty years earlier abortion up to twenty-four weeks was legalized, and the city that provided the most abortions in the country. Remember, on the Jewish calendar the Jubilee takes place every fifty years, and it is a time of return, restoration, and restitution, a time of reckoning for what has been stolen. New York was also ground zero for the battle to remove prayer from schools. But it was also New York City where George Washington made a covenant between the nation and God, stating that if the nation ever turned from God, God would turn from them.

The World Health Organization, Anthony Fauci, deep-state leaders (including some who were positioned in the church for this very time), and a company of local and regional players all began to put forth their revelations that had no true scientific backing and were meant to instill *fear* in the minds of the nation's citizens. They herded them like cattle, locked them down, and rolled out a ruthless plan to inject toxic potions into humanity. Once again, the company of the prophets of Baal and Ashtoreth were out as mockingbirds, along with the colosseum of media and technology: wear masks; stay six feet apart; don't leave your homes; you must be vaccinated to help protect others; if you refuse you are murdering people. The spirit of fear was released upon the nation.

Fear never works alone. It always works with a team. Demons operate in packs like wolves, and this was no different. The spirit of fear works in tandem with the spirits of control and manipulation. Once fear sets in, it is far easier to control the actions of the people, and then they can be manipulated to believe whatever these forces want them to believe. The plumb line was dropped, dividing the sheep from the goats and the shepherds from the showmen. The question was, Will we be the confessing church, or will we get in line and prop up a spiritual agenda that is diametrically opposed to the Word of God? That same question applies today.

The false prophets of Baal and Ashtoreth had been positioned around President Trump to purposely steer him in a direction the Lord did not want him to go: "Go up, for the Lord will give you the victory." I do not envy President Trump's position at all when this occurred, because confusion like a black mist easily takes over when someone is not anchored in the Word, checking their emotions and blocking their ability to hear God above all in a national crisis. The agents of darkness were mobilized to lure people through fear, misinformation, and lies. They used the same tactics Satan has been using since creation: Mix a little bit of truth in with a whole lot of lie, or just repeat the lie over and over until people begin to believe it's true because of the number of times it has been repeated. And many people believed the lies, even people in the church.

Discernment is one of the most crucial abilities the people of God need to have sharpened, ready, and operating at a high level. Sharpened discernment means one can be in deep waters and know what is lurking there, having the ability to hear the Lord through the noise. A large percentage of the church has shallow roots—easy to trip over, not very deep, and not very strong. When roots are shallow, discernment is low, and the enemy can easily corral you into believing utter deceptions as truth.

It is moments like this when the church must stand in faith, trusting that "when the enemy comes in like a flood, the Spirit of the LORD will lift up a standard against him" (Isa. 59:19, NKJV). James 4:7 says, "Submit to God. Resist the devil and he will flee from you" (NKJV). The church must be grounded in the truth so they will recognize what is false.

COVID did something that people did not expect. It exposed just how much of the church was willing to be like those three thousand pastors who sided with Hitler and the twelve thousand who did not want to get involved. It exposed how much the body of Christ was willing to forsake the Word, shut down their churches, do what wicked federal and state governments were telling them to do, and tolerate whatever restrictions they were given, going along with anything.

Suddenly churches—which are supposed to be spiritual compasses and beacons of truth—were making people wear masks, taking temperatures at the door, and pushing mass vaccination. Part of the church had been groomed for this for a very long time, just as the Pharisees were groomed by Rome to do their bidding and push their corruption on the people in their charge. The church is meant to liberate people through God's Word and the power and authority given to us through Christ Jesus.

I even heard a few governors and spiritual leaders say, "Jesus would have taken the vaccine." Oh, really? Show me where that is in the Bible, because I think it is a load of you-know-what. The devil will always manipulate the Word and use it in a perverse way to put chains on people who do not have a solid foundation in the Word and are not trained to understand the hallmark markings of a counterfeit. Remember, the devil even tried it with Jesus Himself when He was in a weakened state in the wilderness. The enemy came quoting the Word, misusing it for his corrupt purposes. Jesus answered right back with the Word. When the enemy comes against you with his lies and deception, you can't answer back with the Word if you don't know the Word.

In the midst of COVID, vaccine rollouts, masks, social distancing, and the demonization of ivermectin, two prophetically profound things happened.

A company named Gilead Sciences arose with its own revelation, its own revelationary cure. A drug called remdesivir was rolled out. In trials this drug had been shown to cause serious issues, including kidney failure and respiratory failure, causing respiratory issues to worsen and leading to patients needing to be put on a ventilator.[4] I remember podcaster Dr. Bryan Ardis saying remdesivir stands for run, death is near. However, the enemy utilized Gilead for a very specific reason, appearing to be rising up with a cure.

The balm of Gilead is mentioned in the Book of Jeremiah, when through Jeremiah the Lord asks, "Is there no balm in Gilead, is there no physician there? Why then is there no recovery for the health of the daughter of my people?" (Jer. 8:22, NKJV). The prophet Jeremiah was commissioned by God to warn the southern kingdom of Judah that Jerusalem would be overtaken if they didn't repent of their idolatry and wickedness and return to God. Repentance is a repeating theme within Jeremiah. The prophet endeavored for decades to persuade Judah to repent. Jeremiah is known as the "weeping prophet," for he carried great sorrow because the arrogance of the people was great.

The balm of Gilead is mentioned again in Jeremiah 46:11 as part of the Lord's instructions: "Go up to Gilead and take balm, O virgin, the daughter of Egypt; in vain you will use many medicines; you shall not be cured" (NKJV). He was saying there is no healing for you. Go get balm from Gilead because nothing else will cure you or prevent your judgment from God. God was going to bring His judgment on all nations that went against His will and truths, not just Judah, and Gilead was presented as the only potential source of help when there was no healing for Judah because of their defiance.

The enemy took the connection between Gilead and healing in the Bible and brought the counterfeit Gilead to the forefront in a time when desperate people were searching for a cure to a plague. This is how the enemy puts forth his own revelations that are filled with deceptions, counterfeits, death, and destruction. He takes a little bit of truth—Gilead is a source of a healing balm—and mixes it with a whole lot of lie. Once he is able to release a spirit of fear and get masses to believe the lie, he can easily lure them into following his heinous agenda.

RIP THE BANDAGE OFF

The other highly profound event that occurred in 2020 was a candidate who arose within the Democratic Party to run for president against Donald Trump. Joe Biden, the vice president under Barack Obama for eight years, arose as the American Pharaoh once again for a third term.

On October 17, 2020, at the Democratic National Convention, Vice President Biden said, "This campaign isn't just about winning votes. It's about winning the heart and, yes, the soul of America." The phrase "battle for the soul of America" then appeared right next to his name at the top of his campaign website.[5] Biden was right—it was a battle for the soul of America, and the enemy was determined to win.

Joseph Biden's name should have given a clue as to where this was going. His first and last names together mean he will add from the shadow valley. The nation was about to experience Psalm 23:4: "Even though I walk through the valley of the shadow of death, I fear no evil, for You are with me; Your rod and Your staff, they comfort me" (NASB). Indeed, this circus of players wanted the soul of this nation in chains, in a cell, where they get to be the head jailers.

On October 6, 2020, I delivered a word from the Lord that has become known as "the clash of the titans" word:

> I, the Lord God, am going forth and *rebuking* the wicked, for the persecuting spirit has gone forth; however, the cries from the church are getting greater in number. And it is the church who shall arise with a bullhorn in the midst of chaos, instability, and *fear.* The *core* of the church shall arise and shall shout forth praise to their God! For as *fear* and persecution and uncertainty attempt to march forth, a spirit of boldness shall come upon the remnant of My church, where what they speak, the power that goes forth, is going to arrest whole towns and cities, and a covering of conviction shall go forth and rest upon those areas as people come forth in all humility and surrender to the will of their Creator in heaven, says the Lord of Hosts this day.

The enemy is asking to sift those in leadership and their families like wheat. However, I, the Lord God, have not allowed him his full request. However, I am allowing a certain amount of events to take place in order to humble those before Me who truly need to in all sincerity *surrender*!

Know, My children, as in an airplane there may come a point where that plane enters turbulence and it is bumpy, it is uneasy, there is a lot of movement. However, the pilot is still steering the plane, trained to navigate through such pockets. You may feel the turbulence, it may get bumpy; however, the captain, an experienced captain, knows exactly how to navigate the plane and its passengers through such rough terrain. In the same way, My children, you are entering some turbulence, and it may feel bumpy and uneasy. Things may get tossed about; *however I, the Lord your God, am still navigating you through, and this pocket of turbulence is just that!* I, the Lord, shall lead you through such events where you will see much shaking occurring as events unfold and take place.

There shall be a clash of the titans in Washington, DC, the likes of which has never been seen, historic, says the Lord of Hosts this day. However, in clashes there shall come forth casualties, and there shall be those exposed in both parties who have been liaisons for wicked interests of foreign entities, says the Lord of Hosts this day, *both parties.* And a core shall arise and come forth, a core that fights and stands for truth, My word of truth, says the Lord. My truth shall go forth in the midst and expose a chain gang of players all working together to overthrow not only the foundation of the United States of America *but* all sense of morality and faith in God. They are looking for a

demolition, says the Lord, and a demolition they shall
receive upon their own heads. Watch and see, says the
Lord of Hosts this day!

The trumpet will sound. The trumpet will sound.
In the midst the trumpet will sound, says the Lord,
for I, the Lord, am making an unexpected move that
will catch the enemy, his alliance, and those involved
in the darkest of dealings off guard, off-kilter; a *surprise attack* shall pierce and puncture their plans. They
will draw their own blood, for those spirits they have
been conjuring and calling upon are out for blood and
[are] highly competitive. My children, this is where
you shall see the most shocking infighting occurring
within groups. There is one major player in particular
who shall publicly fall fast and hard, branded for what
they are, says the Lord of Hosts this day.

A rival nominee shall arise, a false convert, one
who would do the bidding of the wicked on the bench.
Watch for this name to be dropped. There will be an
unprecedented counter on the part of the corrupt that
will infuriate their own party and shake even more
from their slumber.

When the Lord used the word *turbulence*, I knew we were
entering a very bumpy and uneasy period, which meant the
election was not going to go as many thought it would. And
that is exactly what happened. Let me make this very clear:
The Lord allowed 2020 to happen. He allowed it, and He
allowed it because there would have been even more division.
The 2016 election was about purposely dividing a nation; in
2020 it would have been even worse if Donald Trump had
taken office again. The 2020 election was like ripping a bandage off, a very large bandage that had been hiding a deep
infection in the nation. In 2020 the Lord ripped the bandage

off and allowed all the ugliness to ooze out to show the people how great a stench the sin, the corruptness, and the deception truly was.

The serpent of wokeism reared up for a strike. Remember, wokeism goes back to the serpent at the tree of the knowledge of good and evil. It is the same playbook, reworked to bring a modern-day revelation. The same corrupted root sprouted man-eating plants that rapidly grew and began seeking to consume men and women and swallow them up into their agendas, making their own revelations known across the airwaves, infiltrating the schools, and slithering into the churches. COVID-19 groomed the woke churches, the lukewarm churches, so that they would surrender to these agendas and the church would then be doing the enemy's bidding.

Yet in the midst of the continuing lies about COVID, with unprotected borders and undocumented gang members of military fighting age coming in like a flood, drug trafficking hitting new alarming levels, sex traffickers with open access crossing the border, and terrorist groups sending their disciples across the border, in the midst of the oppression bearing down on the nation, something revelationary occurred. On June 24, 2022, in the middle of a highly liberal administration in power in the White House, *Roe v. Wade* was overturned. It was almost fifty years after the original decision. The decision sent shock waves through the nation.

The Lord does not need a majority to raise a standard against and defeat evil. He requires a faithful, obedient minority because when that minority submits to and partners with almighty God, it becomes the majority. *Roe v. Wade* proved that when the Supreme Court justices acted righteously, in accordance with the law.

911

January 27, 2023, I had a word from the Lord:

> And the Spirit of the Lord says this day, they shall come with chains and fetters to bind you, and if you humbly come to Me, I shall break their chains of iron. Their charges shall befall them, for they have been doing even worse in the dark behind the door to the inner chamber.

In early 2023 I was in Tulsa, Oklahoma, to minister and stay with friends. I was awoken at midnight by the Lord and told:

> Donald trump was the forty-fifth president. He is running to be the forty-seventh president.
> $4 + 5 = 9, 4 + 7 = 11$
> 911, 911!

On March 17, 2023, I received another word from the Lord:

> However, a fall off a high seat shall leave those unable to continue in their half charade, bait and switch, bait and switch, says the Lord, indict and switch at the same time. This shall be attempted, says the Lord.

On March 27, 2023, a horrific school shooting occurred in Nashville. A transgender individual killed three children and three adults at the Covenant School. The name of the school was *Covenant*!

The Lord said to me, "The covenant is under attack!" The word with 911 was the warning of the political, spiritual, and foundational attack that was about to be launched in this nation—guerrilla warfare in a digital arena, and lawfare within the judicial branch. The covenant is legal and binding to the Lord. It is ever active. When God's people humble themselves and come under the yoke, an attack on an active covenant has always resulted in a spectacular downfall of the wicked and the blasphemers.

In March 2023 the first indictment of Donald Trump came down as well. "They are coming to bind you with fetters. Here we go," I thought.

On October 7, 2023, Israel's 911 happened. The Lord had said 911. Israel and the United States are connected by a vein in the realm of the Spirit. Therefore, the enemy would set his sights on the covenant God made with Israel as well. One day after the Jubilee, or fifty-year anniversary of the Yom Kippur war, Hamas launched a barbaric attack on Israel, declaring war over, among other things, red heifers that had arrived in Israel. A revelationary war indeed.

Genesis 6:11 states, "Now the earth was corrupt in the sight of God, and the earth was filled with violence" (NASB). The word *violence* in Hebrew is *ḥāmās*.[6] Hamas means violence. The spirit of Amalek—Israel's oldest enemy, a spirit of death, destruction, and hatred that is intent on destroying Israel—has risen up again, as it does in every generation. First Peter 5:8 says, "Be sober [well balanced and self-disciplined], be alert and cautious at all times. That enemy of yours, the devil, prowls around like a roaring lion [fiercely hungry], seeking someone to devour."

The Hamas attack on Israel came after the Biden administration, in their own twisted revelation, thought it would be a brilliant idea to give Iran six billion dollars. Iran supports Hamas and uses Hamas as a proxy. The spirit of Amalek entered the United States and utilized Generation Z and universities that have become temples of Baal and Marxism to do its bidding. Remember, in the 1930s in Germany, protests against Jews broke out at universities across the country, and

Jewish students were driven out. The same thing happened in the United States in 2024, with anti-Semitic protests and discrimination and violence against Jewish students. The *New York Post* reported, "Jewish students at Columbia University were chased out of their dorms, received death threats, spat upon, stalked and pinned against walls."[7]

The mutated sword of Amalek had returned, with Black Lives Matter, LGBTQ+ groups, socialist professors, woke students, and paid protesters all coming together to support not only Palestine but Hamas.

CHAPTER 12

THE CHALLENGE AND THE CHOICE

THE REVELATIONARY WAR reached a fever pitch heading into 2024.

With an election coming, false prophets made a lot of noise. They have a hallmark, one that is easy to spot. False prophets steer you away from the things of God, away from reverence, away from holiness, away from Jesus Christ, and false prophets try to convince people to put their hope and faith in a man or in a movement. The true prophets of God point you right back to Jesus Christ.

The prophets of the media were like a digital army, attempting to prop up a puppet in Biden, thinking that if they repeated the lie enough that he was mentally fit, we would actually believe it. We didn't, which is why he was replaced with Kamala Harris. They were also painting Donald Trump to be the most heinous individual ever. Christians were being painted as right-wing extremists and nationalists because they stood for godliness, life, and morality. But as always, when we voted for a leader of this nation, we were not voting for a pastor. Abraham, Joseph, Moses, David, and Jehu were all very flawed men, but the Lord saw something deep within them that man could not see. However, we must always remember that a man cannot save America; only almighty God can.

THE CROSSROADS

On December 11, 2023, I had a word from the Lord:

> Thus says the Lord, the Rose Garden. Just watch, says
> the Lord, the events that unfold and what is spoken out
> of such a place that has many thorns hidden in such
> bushes, says the Lord. Time is short, leaders. To repent,
> time is short. A bait and switch, says the Lord, a bait
> and switch. Watch for the subtleties, says the Lord.
> Watch for them. Some are trading their sons for their
> positions, says the Lord. They are putting their sons on
> the wall as a sacrifice.

I had warned going into 2024 that we were entering 5784 on the Jewish calendar, which translated to the prison doors opening to Joseph. Well, for prison doors to open, sometimes they have to close first.

During the first half of 2024 many historic and prophetic events occurred as the revelationary war raged on. March 31, 2024—Easter, the day we celebrate the resurrection of Jesus Christ—was also Transgender Day of Visibility, first declared and celebrated in 2009. As if we did not see the perversion enough to begin with! This was the enemy's clear revelation of a counterfeit to be celebrated on the day of Jesus' resurrection. Jesus died for these people to become delivered and set free, not to be given more press.

On April 5, 2024, there was an earthquake with the epicenter located near Whitehouse Station, New Jersey, about seven miles from the Trump National Golf Club Bedminster. The earthquake went up through New York, and boy, did we feel it! The earthquake was magnitude 4.8, and three days later, on April 8, 2024, a total solar eclipse passed over two towns in North America named Nineveh, one in Indiana and one in Ohio. Nineveh is where the prophet Jonah pronounced that judgment was coming in forty days—causing the people of Nineveh to repent.

Biblical plagues of insects descended upon the United States, including trillions of cicadas, the likes of which have not been seen since 1803 when the Louisiana Purchase happened. There was also an invasion of spongy moth caterpillars that were eating all vegetation. I witnessed this firsthand living in upstate New York.

Passover was at the end of April. On the second full day of Passover, Big Ben—the iconic clock in London—froze.[1] The Lord showed me that when Ben stops, Benjamin stops and Judah begins. Saul was from the tribe of Benjamin, and when the reign of Saul came to an end, the reign of David, who was from the tribe of Judah, began. This was prophetically signaling a very serious and vast changing of the guard in the earth's leadership that would affect nations and churches. A bait and switch was coming, as well as turbulence after Passover.

Not long after this, a string of resignations occurred in the leadership of the country and in church leadership. The two happened in tandem. The dividing line between the showmen and the shepherds went even further, as judgment begins in the house of God.

On May 30, 2024, Trump was convicted on thirty-four counts of falsifying business records. The trial was as much a trial of the American people as it was of Donald Trump. Had he never come back to run for president again, the political hunt would never have happened.

There is a divide in the church about Trump and who he is. The Lord knows the heart and the motive. The Lord chose him for another term, and I believe *he will be yoked by God*. The most successful leaders in the Bible wore the yoke!

When they attempted to throw off the yoke, they got themselves in much trouble and placed the nation in jeopardy.

With the results of the 2024 election there is a historic opportunity in this nation. This time around, Trump, the one who holds the highest seat, *must* wear that biblical yoke. The many layers of deception in the nation must be dealt with at the root and torn up by the insight and wisdom only the Lord almighty can give.

Our nation stands at a crossroads. A core has risen up within the fivefold ministry, a seasoned core, a core of prophets who have been steadfast in speaking the word of the Lord to a very sick nation instead of being glorified cheerleaders spoon-feeding sour milk and stale bread to the church. The *meat* is required in such a time as this. The meat helps the church to grow and endure. And for the meat to be spoken and consumed, the prophetic must come out deeper—the Lord is requiring it.

THE CHALLENGE

In this present day we find ourselves living in an identity-swallowing culture, just as the prophet Daniel found himself in the identity-swallowing culture of Babylon. The challenge in such an environment is to maintain your identity in Christ as a born-again, blood-bought, Spirit-filled believer, grounded in the Word, walking in freedom, and worshipping the Lord in spirit and in truth.

There is a reason we see the gospel thriving and the church rapidly growing in countries where the gospel is outlawed. You can't be lukewarm when you might go to jail or be killed for your faith. We are in this world, but we are not of this world. Our citizenship is in heaven. Even when wickedness, paganism, and idolatry attempt to swallow the gospel, the gospel has the power to enlighten and transform lives in a way that false religions do not.

Your identity in Christ needs to transcend culture—even American church culture—and the current condition of the nation, regardless of who the leader is. Another way to say it is your identity needs to eclipse the culture.

When Daniel was taken captive to Babylon, he faced a challenge. He had a choice to make. He could follow God's Law, putting his life in danger, or he could just go along with the culture and stay "safe." Daniel met the challenge: "But Daniel purposed in his heart that he would not defile himself" (Dan. 1:8, NKJV).

His decision was based on love and devotion to God, serving Him even in the hostile Babylonian environment. His decision was based on faith; the decision could result in suffering, but he knew God could sustain him. His decision was based on the fear of God; he cared more about what God thought than what his captors and the king thought, for they had no power over his soul. His decision was based on humility, and it was private. It was not announced to everyone else in the court.

The challenge is, Will you do the same? Ask yourselves, With what is happening in the nation, how firm is my identity in Christ?

Godly resolve in our own lives begins with the small things—serving God in private with no one looking. When no one is looking, will you do what God is asking you to do just because He asked?

One of the things we can take away from the story of Daniel is when you gain victory in the small and private areas of your life, when your resolve grows and with it your obedience to do what He is asking you to do, the Lord can do exceedingly, abundantly above what you ever ask or imagine. Watch what the Lord can do with that; He can increase in ways you never thought possible from such a foundation. I went through private conditioning and trials for seventeen years before the Lord ever allowed me to speak a word publicly.

This is an excerpt from a word of the Lord from May 3, 2021:

> Do you truly think, My children, that this battle in your nation is beyond Me, is beyond My power? Put your faith in *Me* and *My plan*, *My timing*, knowing My power is infinite, and that I sit on the throne, as the earth is *My* footstool, says the Lord of Hosts. Your circumstances and what you face in your lives and in this nation is *not* too difficult for Me, for I am your strong tower and refuge in times of trouble. I am far above every power, principality, or might. I will keep those in perfect peace whose mind is stayed on Me, even in an hour where darkness is making a huge push, where the enemy is attempting a strong advance. I, the Lord your God, have the final *word*.

When we head into environments that may not be favorable toward Christians, we must remember we are called to be leaders and servants. God has called us to stand out because we belong to Him. His light in us is meant to be in dark areas to begin to drive away the darkness because God's sacred order of time is that darkness must give way to the light. The greater the darkness, the greater each little piece of light becomes. A small light can burst through and illuminate the darkness, expose what is there, and drive it out.

Isaiah 11:2 says, "And the Spirit of the LORD will rest on Him—the Spirit of wisdom and understanding, the Spirit of counsel and strength, the Spirit of knowledge and of the [reverential and obedient] fear of the Lord." In an identity-swallowing culture, in a culture that is hostile to believers, in a society that more and more teaches witchcraft, astrology, and the ways of the dark arts to the young, the Spirit of counsel, wisdom, and knowledge that comes from God Most High has the authority and power to cut through all that like a double-edged sword and expose the *truth*.

THE CHOICE

Even amid witch hunts and media cauldrons, we who hold the prophetic office and others within the fivefold ministry *must* go out deeper with the Lord and learn to handle the pressure in the deep end. Those who are profiting from splashing around in the shallow end and making a lot of noise—being showmen rather than shepherds—will be left in a muddy puddle. As we go through this process as a nation, the prophetic will be sanitized where it has been muddied and treated as a circus act by the immature and shallow. The year 2024 was a year of pruning and new growth, and with that comes growing pains for the nation, the church, and individuals.

The year 2024 was the year of Joshua 24 for the nation and the church:

> "Now, therefore, fear the LORD and serve Him in sincerity and truth; and put away the gods which your fathers served beyond the River and in Egypt, and serve the LORD. If it is disagreeable in your sight to serve the LORD, choose for yourselves today whom you will serve: whether the gods which your fathers served which were beyond the River, or the gods of the Amorites in whose land you are living; but as for me and my house, we will serve the LORD."
>
> The people answered and said, "Far be it from us that we should forsake the LORD to serve other gods;

for the LORD our God is He who brought us and our fathers up out of the land of Egypt....We also will serve the LORD, for He is our God."

Then Joshua said to the people, "You will not be able to serve the LORD, for He is a holy God. He is a jealous God; He will not forgive your transgression or your sins. If you forsake the LORD and serve foreign gods, then He will turn and do you harm and consume you after He has done good to you." The people said to Joshua, "No, but we will serve the LORD." Joshua said to the people, "You are witnesses against yourselves that you have chosen for yourselves the LORD, to serve Him." And they said, "We are witnesses."

"Now therefore, put away the foreign gods which are in your midst, and incline your hearts to the LORD, the God of Israel." The people said to Joshua, "We will serve the LORD our God and we will obey His voice." So Joshua made a covenant with the people that day, and made for them a statute and an ordinance in Shechem. And Joshua wrote these words in the book of the law of God; and he took a large stone and set it up there under the oak that was by the sanctuary of the LORD. Joshua said to all the people, "Behold, this stone shall be for a witness against us, for it has heard all the words of the LORD which He spoke to us; thus it shall be for a witness against you, so that you do not deny your God."

—JOSHUA 24:14–27, NASB

Joshua stood before the people and gave them a choice and the consequence for turning from the Lord, just as Elijah stood on Mount Carmel, facing the prophets of Baal and Ashtoreth, and called the people of Israel to account (1 Kings 18). We can no longer falter between two opinions. Just as the people of Israel had to choose whom they would serve, we have to choose whom we will serve.

This is a message to America, the church, and the people in leadership in the highest seats in the land: *Why do you falter between two opinions? Choose this day whom you will serve. If God be God, serve Him in spirit and in truth. If Baal is God, then chase after such delusions, and such will be your wage!*

The prophetic is meant to be divisive, to divide the truth of God's Word from the lie. An all-too-significant part of the church currently is in direct opposition to God and His Word; they have positioned themselves to counteract what the church is truly meant to do.

The high places need to be torn down, and the altars of the Lord must be rebuilt in their place! We are soldiers in the army of the living God. Those of us in the prophetic and fivefold ministry are not meant to be motivational speakers with feel-good megaphones. We are meant to speak the word of the Lord in all truth, expose the works of darkness and iniquity, and point people back to almighty God. We need to speak forth that a relationship with almighty God through Jesus Christ is their salvation—not a man, not a political leader, not a church building, but Jesus Christ, the King of kings and Lord of lords!

Martin Luther King Jr. stated in his "I Have a Dream" speech:

> I am not unmindful that some of you have come here out of great trials and tribulations. Some of you have come fresh from narrow jail cells. Some of you have come from areas where your quest for freedom left you battered by the storms of persecution....You have been the veterans of creative suffering. Continue to work with the faith that unearned suffering is redemptive.[2]

Continue to be diligent in the face of trials and tribulations. Raise the standard, put your hand to the plow, and be diligent in your faith—for "without faith it is impossible to please Him, for he who comes to God must believe that He is and that He is a rewarder of those who seek Him" (Heb. 11:6, NASB).

NOTES

CHAPTER 1

1. *Star Wars: A New Hope*, directed by George Lucas (1977).
2. *Merriam-Webster*, s.v. "edify," accessed November 25, 2024, https://www.merriam-webster.com/dictionary/edify.
3. Blue Letter Bible, s.v. "*oikodomeō*," accessed November 25, 2024, https://www.blueletterbible.org/lexicon/g3618/kjv/tr/0-1/.

CHAPTER 2

1. *Merriam-Webster*, s.v. "truth," accessed November 26, 2024, https://www.merriam-webster.com/dictionary/truth.
2. *Collins English Dictionary*, s.v. "truth," accessed November 26, 2024, https://www.collinsdictionary.com/us/dictionary/english/truth.
3. Bible Study Tools, s.v. "Truth," accessed November 26, 2024, https://www.biblestudytools.com/dictionary/truth/.
4. Oswald Chambers, *Devotions for a Deeper Life* (Zondervan, 2009), 171.
5. Chambers, *Devotions for a Deeper Life*, 171.
6. *Merriam-Webster*, s.v. "witness," accessed November 26, 2024, https://www.merriam-webster.com/dictionary/witness.
7. Blue Letter Bible, s.v. "*šāmar*," accessed November 27, 2024, https://www.blueletterbible.org/lexicon/h8104/kjv/wlc/0-1/.
8. Oswald Chambers, *The Complete Works of Oswald Chambers* (Our Daily Bread Publishing, 2013), 537.

CHAPTER 3

1. Blue Letter Bible, s.v. "*nāḥaš*," accessed November 29, 2024, https://www.blueletterbible.org/lexicon/h5172/kjv/wlc/0-1/.
2. *Cambridge Dictionary*, s.v. "deflection," accessed November 29, 2024, https://dictionary.cambridge.org/us/dictionary/english/deflection.

CHAPTER 4

1. Aaron L. Raskin, "Tzadik," Chabad.org, accessed November 30, 2024, https://www.chabad.org/library/article_cdo/aid/137090/jewish/Tzadik.htm.

CHAPTER 5

1. Kim Clement, *Call Me Crazy, but I'm Hearing God* (Destiny Image, 2007), 50, 53.
2. Donné Clement Petruska, "Kim Clement 9/11 Prophecy—Part 1," Subsplash, September 23, 2019, https://subsplash.com/+1d45/embed/mi/+q8c9qjx?video&audio&info&embeddable&shareable&logo_watermark.
3. Kim Clement (@officialkimclement), "Kim Clement Trump 2 Terms Prophecy—Feb 22nd, 2007," Instagram reel, October 28, 2024, https://www.instagram.com/officialkimclement/reel/DBrO0zpC9JN/.
4. Hierophant, "This Video Proves Kim Clement Is a True Prophet of God—February 22, 2014," YouTube, March 28, 2022, https://www.youtube.com/watch?v=dOMayU-sBuo.

CHAPTER 6

1. Kim Clement, "Prophecy," House of Destiny, November 5, 2012, https://www.houseofdestiny.org/prophecy/word/?trid=468.

CHAPTER 7

1. "Billy Graham on Communism: 'Satan's Religion' (1954)," Alpha History, accessed December 4, 2024, https://alphahistory.com/coldwar/billy-graham-communism-satans-religion-1954/.
2. "Media (Region)," Wikipedia, accessed December 4, 2024, https://en.wikipedia.org/wiki/Media_(region)#.
3. TOI Staff, "Yuval Noah Harari Warns AI Can Create Religious Texts, May Inspire New Cults," The Times of Israel, May 3, 2023, https://www.timesofisrael.com/yuval-noah-harari-warns-ai-can-create-religious-texts-may-inspire-new-cults/.
4. "Operation Mockingbird," Wikipedia, updated September 2, 2024, https://en.wikipedia.org/wiki/Operation_Mockingbird.
5. Deborah Davis, *Katharine the Great* (Sheridan Square Press, 1991), xii–xxi.

6. "Mockingbird," Wikipedia, updated October 16, 2024, https://en.wikipedia.org/wiki/Mockingbird.

7. *Merriam-Webster*, s.v. "censor," accessed December 5, 2024, https://www.merriam-webster.com/dictionary/censor.

8. *Merriam-Webster*, s.v. "suppress," accessed December 5, 2024, https://www.merriam-webster.com/dictionary/suppress.

9. Dan Bilefsky, "Move Over Moses and Zoroaster: Manhattan Has a New Female Lawgiver," *New York Times*, updated January 27, 2023, https://www.nytimes.com/2023/01/25/arts/design/discrimination-sculpture-madison-park-sikander-women.html.

10. Mike Gonzalez, "Yes, a Pro-China Group in America Supports a Black Lives Matter Founder," The Heritage Foundation, October 21, 2020, https://www.heritage.org/progressivism/commentary/yes-pro-china-group-america-supports-black-lives-matter-founder.

11. Maria Morava and Scottie Andrew, "The Black Lives Matter Foundation Raised $90 Million in 2020, and Gave Almost a Quarter of It to Local Chapters and Organizations," CNN, February 25, 2021, https://www.cnn.com/2021/02/25/us/black-lives-matter-2020-donation-report-trnd/index.html#.

12. William Lawyer, "What Organizations Fund Planned Parenthood?," Human Life International, accessed December 6, 2024, https://www.hli.org/resources/list-of-who-supports-planned-parenthood/.

13. Jay Greene et al., "Protecting American Universities from Undue Foreign Influence," The Heritage Foundation, February 13, 2024, https://www.heritage.org/education/report/protecting-american-universities-undue-foreign-influence#.

14. "Aleister Crowley," Wikipedia, updated November 3, 2024, https://en.wikipedia.org/wiki/Aleister_Crowley.

15. "Aleister Crowley," Wikipedia.

16. *Merriam-Webster*, s.v. "tolerance," accessed December 8, 2024, https://www.merriam-webster.com/dictionary/tolerance.

17. *Merriam-Webster*, s.v. "indulge," accessed December 8, 2024, https://www.merriam-webster.com/dictionary/indulge.

CHAPTER 8

1. Jonathan Cahn, *The Book of Mysteries* (FrontLine, 2018), 36.

CHAPTER 9

1. "Billy Graham on Communism," Alpha History.
2. "Declaration of Independence," National Archives, July 4, 1776, https://www.archives.gov/founding-docs/declaration-transcript.
3. Rudy Giuliani, quoted in "A Plan to Save the World Trade Center," Twin Towers Alliance, updated July 17, 2011, https://twintowersalliance.com/save-the-wtc/; George W. Bush, "Address to a Joint Session of Congress and the American People," The White House, September 20, 2001, https://georgewbush-whitehouse.archives.gov/news/releases/2001/09/20010920-8.html.
4. "Congressional Record—Senate," US Congress, September 12, 2001, https://www.congress.gov/crec/2001/09/12/CREC-2001-09-12-pt1-PgS9284.pdf.
5. Peter Gay, *Weimar Culture: The Outsider as Insider* (W. W. Norton, 2001), 6.
6. *Encyclopaedia Britannica*, s.v. "Weimar Republic," updated October 15, 2024, https://www.britannica.com/place/Weimar-Republic/The-end-of-the-Weimar-Republic.
7. *Encyclopaedia Britannica*, s.v. "Weimar Republic."
8. Kurt Struckmeyer, "The Complicity of Moderates in Nazi Germany," Following Jesus, February 2, 2020, https://followingjesus.org/the-complicity-of-moderates-in-nazi-germany/.
9. Martin Niemöller, "First They Came For…," Holocaust Encyclopedia, accessed November 10, 2024, https://encyclopedia.ushmm.org/content/en/article/martin-niemoeller-first-they-came-for-the-socialists.
10. "The Nazis and the Altar of Satan," Christian Friends of Israel, accessed November 10, 2024, https://cfi-usa.org/pergamon-to-berlin/.
11. Abigail Eisenstadt, "The True Story Behind How Pearls Are Made," *Smithsonian*, August 5, 2021, https://www.smithsonianmag.com/blogs/national-museum-of-natural-history/2021/08/05/true-story-behind-how-pearls-are-made/.
12. Max Fisher, "The Emperor's Speech: 67 Years Ago, Hirohito Transformed Japan Forever," *The Atlantic*, August 15, 2012, https://www.theatlantic.com/international/archive/2012/08/the-emperors-speech-67-years-ago-hirohito-transformed-japan-forever/261166/.

13. Karl Marx, "The Fiddler," Marxists, accessed November 10, 2024, https://www.marxists.org/archive/marx/works/1837-pre/verse/verse4.htm.

14. Paul Kengor, "86—Karl Marx, 'Monster of Ten Thousand Devils,'" Catholic Culture Podcast, September 29, 2020, https://catholicculturepodcast.libsyn.com/86-karl-marx-monster-of-ten-thousand-devils-paul-kengor.

15. "Engel v. Vitale, 370 U.S. 421 (1962)," Justia, June 25, 1962, https://supreme.justia.com/cases/federal/us/370/421/#tab-opinion-1943886.

16. "Ethical Movement," Wikipedia, updated October 30, 2024, https://en.wikipedia.org/wiki/Ethical_movement#In_America.

17. Chambers, *Devotions for a Deeper Life*, 99.

CHAPTER 10

1. "Transcript of Barack Obama's Victory Speech," NPR, November 5, 2008, https://www.npr.org/2008/11/05/96624326/transcript-of-barack-obamas-victory-speech.

2. Charles Spurgeon, "The Treasury of David—Psalm 39," Spurgeon Archive, accessed November 11, 2024, http://www.romans45.org/spurgeon/treasury/ps039.htm.

3. "Read Martin Luther King Jr.'s 'I Have a Dream' Speech in Its Entirety," NPR, updated January 16, 2023, https://www.npr.org/2010/01/18/122701268/i-have-a-dream-speech-in-its-entirety.

4. "Great Recession," Wikipedia, updated September 24, 2024, https://simple.wikipedia.org/wiki/Great_Recession#.

5. Josh Earnest, "Beam Signed by President Obama Installed at World Trade Center," The White House, August 2, 2012, https://obamawhitehouse.archives.gov/blog/2012/08/02/beam-signed-president-obama-installed-world-trade-center.

6. Carrie Budoff Brown, "Obama Says Marriage Is Between Man and Woman," *Politico*, August 16, 2008, https://www.politico.com/blogs/ben-smith/2008/08/obama-says-marriage-is-between-man-and-woman-011026.

7. Louis Jacobson, "Planned Parenthood Says Obama Promised to 'Put Reproductive Health Care at the Center' of Health Reform," Politifact, November 10, 2009, https://www.politifact.

com/factchecks/2009/nov/10/planned-parenthood/planned-parenthood-says-obama-promised-put-reprodu/.

8. Paraphrasing "Aleister Crowley," Wikipedia.

9. "Read Obama's Speech About Same-Sex Marriage Ruling," *Time*, June 26, 2015, https://time.com/3937925/obama-speech-same-sex-marriage/.

CHAPTER 11

1. Kim Clement, "Kim Clement Trump 2 Terms Prophecy Fulfilled—2024," YouTube, November 6, 2024, https://www.youtube.com/watch?v=VpG7os6AqX8&t=4s.

2. *Merriam-Webster*, s.v. "rod," accessed November 1, 2024, https://www.merriam-webster.com/dictionary/rod.

3. "Potential Links Between the Wuhan Institute of Virology and the Origin of the COVID-19 Pandemic," Office of the Director of National Intelligence, June 2023, https://www.dni.gov/files/ODNI/documents/assessments/Report-on-Potential-Links-Between-the-Wuhan-Institute-of-Virology-and-the-Origins-of-COVID-19-20230623.pdf.

4. "FAQ: Remdesivir Formulation and Adverse Events," Duke University School of Medicine, May 29, 2020, https://dason.medicine.duke.edu/sites/default/files/remdesivir_formulations_and_adverse_events_faq_0.pdf; Jonathan Grein et al., "Compassionate Use of Remdesivir for Patients with Severe COVID-19," *New England Journal of Medicine* 382, no. 24 (2020): 2327–36, https://doi.org/10.1056/NEJMoa2007016.

5. Elizabeth Dias, "Biden and Trump Say They're Fighting for America's 'Soul.' What Does That Mean?," *New York Times*, October 17, 2020, https://www.nytimes.com/2020/10/17/us/biden-trump-soul-nation-country.html.

6. Blue Letter Bible, s.v. "ḥāmās," accessed November 12, 2024, https://www.blueletterbible.org/lexicon/h2555/kjv/wlc/0-1/.

7. Matthew Sedacca, "Jewish Columbia Students Were Chased Out of Dorms, Spat On, and Pinned Against Walls," *New York Post*, August 31, 2024, https://nypost.com/2024/08/31/us-news/columbia-antisemitism-task-force-details-student-assaults-targeting-after-oct-7/.

CHAPTER 12

1. Harry Howard, "Big Ben's Hands Freeze at 9am for More Than an Hour…," DailyMail.com, April 24, 2024, https://www.dailymail.co.uk/news/article-13344577/Big-Ben-Westminster-clock-stops-working.html.
2. "Read Martin Luther King Jr.'s 'I Have a Dream' Speech in Its Entirety," NPR.

ABOUT THE AUTHOR

AMANDA GRACE IS a prophetic teacher and the founder of Ark of Grace Ministries. With a deep love for the Lord and a passion for sharing His prophetic insights, she has dedicated her life to guiding individuals in their spiritual journeys. Through her teachings and ministry Amanda Grace imparts wisdom, encourages spiritual growth, and empowers believers to discover and walk in their divine destinies. Her commitment to biblical teachings and her heart for helping others make her a respected leader in the prophetic community. Amanda Grace's ministry inspires and transforms lives, bringing hope, healing, and deeper understanding of God's love and purpose.

Made in the USA
Las Vegas, NV
31 March 2025

20329520R00125